RECORDS
OF
SPORT IN SOUTHERN INDIA

RECORDS

OF

SPORT IN SOUTHERN INDIA

CHIEFLY ON THE

ANNAMULLAY, NIELGHERRY AND PULNEY MOUNTAINS

ALSO INCLUDING NOTES ON

SINGAPORE, JAVA AND LABUAN

FROM JOURNALS WRITTEN BETWEEN 1844 AND 1870

DOUGLAS HAMILTON

EDITOR

EDWARD HAMILTON

GYAN

Published by

GYAN

Gyan Publishing House
5, Ansari Road
Daryaganj, New Delhi-110002
Phone: 011-47034999, 9811692060
E-mail: books@gyanbooks.com

Distribution Network
gyanbooks.com
India, USA, Canada, UK, Australia

ISBN: 978-93-6780-202-1 (HB)

First Published, 1892

2nd Impression 2024

Printed at: Gyan Press, Delhi.

RECORDS OF SPORT IN SOUTHERN INDIA
Author: DOUGLAS HAMILTON

RECORDS

OF

SPORT IN SOUTHERN INDIA.

(1870.)

RECORDS

OF

SPORT IN SOUTHERN INDIA

CHIEFLY ON THE

ANNAMULLAY, NIELGHERRY AND PULNEY MOUNTAINS

Also including Notes on

SINGAPORE, JAVA AND LABUAN

FROM JOURNALS WRITTEN BETWEEN 1844 AND 1870

BY THE LATE

GENERAL DOUGLAS HAMILTON

MADRAS ARMY.

WITH PORTRAIT AND ILLUSTRATIONS FROM HIS ORIGINAL SKETCHES

EDITED BY HIS BROTHER,

EDWARD HAMILTON, M.D., F.L.S., F.Z.S.

London

R. H. PORTER,

18, PRINCES STREET, CAVENDISH SQUARE, W.

1892

PREFACE.

"'Why have you not written a book about your sporting adventures?'" is a question often asked me by my friends when they were looking over my sketch books and I was describing the various scenes. But book writing is not my forte and I have not the slightest pretension to any literary talent. However, during my long illness the subject was again pressed upon me, and I have put together the following pages, extracts from my journals, and have selected from my sketches those which would best illustrate the scenes and adventures described. I am writing of years long gone by when the muzzle loader, with all its drawbacks, was the chief weapon in use."

I found the above portion of an unfinished preface amongst my brother's papers. I have endeavoured to carry out his wishes by publishing his notes almost precisely as he had written them, adding occasionally from his journals and sketches, when found necessary, for the purpose of concluding a half-told tale.

I have been most kindly assisted, particularly as regards the Indian names of localities, &c., by my brother's old and valued friend, General James Michael, C.S.I.

All the illustrations (with the exception of three) are taken from my brother's sketch books. Those which he drew in Indian ink have, by means of *photo-etching*, been transferred as *facsimiles*. The remaining were sketched in pencil, and not being suitable to this process have been copied by Mr. J. T. Smit with such care and accuracy that he has completely caught the touch, as well as the spirit, of the original sketches. The three plates of the two species of Florikin and of the Jungle Cat are from drawings made expressly for this work by Mr. J. T. Smit.

To Mr. R. H. Porter, the publisher, I return my best thanks for the great attention he has paid to the printing and other accessories so necessary to place the work before the subscribers and general public in a satisfactory form.

EDWARD HAMILTON.

December, 1892.

Sketched by Lieut Colonel Douglas Hamilton, Madras Army

WATERFALL NEAR THE VILLAGE OF KILLEYOR.

DOUGLAS HAMILTON, the youngest of eight sons of Charles Hamilton of Sudbury Grove, Middlesex, and of Kensworth House, Herts, was born on the 8th of April, 1818, and was educated at Harrow School. In 1834 he went to Addiscombe, and received his commission in the Indian Army in 1837, being gazetted to the 21st Regiment of Madras Native Infantry; embarking at Portsmouth in the "Duke of Argyle" on September 1st of the same year, and arriving in the Madras Roads on the the 14th December. By the advice of his uncle Captain George Peevor of His Majesty's 17th Foot, who had served in the Nepaul Campaign of 1815-16 and in the Mahratta and Pindaree wars, 1817-18, including the capture of Jubbulpore, he kept a journal from the day he embarked for Madras in 1837 to the day of his death in 1892, and fourteen thick quarto volumes, most carefully written, record all the successes and the failures of his sporting life in India as well as many other interesting events.

In the same Presidency, but his senior in the Service as in years was his brother Richard, a Captain in the 1st Regiment M.N.I., who was afterwards so well known to all Southern Indian sportsmen as the author of "Game" under the soubriquet of "Hawkeye." Although as fond of sport as his elder brother, Douglas Hamilton was, in his younger days, a very indifferent shot, especially with the rifle, and he had to stand a good deal of chaff from his brother officers; but in course of time by dint of patience, perseverance, and determination, he became one of the best rifle shots in the Presidency, and a better sportsman never pulled a trigger.

Although his earliest experience with the rifle was with Antelope as described in the first chapter of these Records, his great ambition was to try his hand and eye on bigger game, and this he was able to do in after years to his heart's content. His well-known Hut near Pykara on the Nielgherries was the rendezvous of many, famous in Indian sporting annals. His first wish was to shew the best sport to all who visited him and his entire abnegation of self was ever conspicuous and thoroughly appreciated.

In 1846 he went with his regiment to Singapore, and was lucky enough to obtain three months' leave to visit the Island of Java, as he describes it, the most beautiful island in the world. He had every hope of obtaining some grand sport, but unfortunately in this though fortunately in every other respect, the Governor of Singapore gave him a special letter of introduction to the Governor General at Batavia; the consequence of this was that from the excessive care they took of him and the dread that any mishap should befall him when out shooting, his great desire of being able to bag a rhinocerous or a Javanese tiger was entirely frustrated, as the shikaries had strict orders never to allow him to get anywhere near either of these beasts. In every other respect his wishes were at once acceded to. He was received with all honours and he was enabled by the means placed at his disposal by the Governor General to visit the greater part of the island, and his descriptions of the temples and excursions to the great volcanoes are full of interest. On his return to Singapore he was sent with his company to Labuan to replace the Marines decimated by fever, and in that Island he remained for some months.

In 1849 he visited England on furlough and returned to India in 1852. He took great interest in the conservation of the Forests in Southern India, and often visited his old friend Michael (now General Michael, C.S.I.) who was organizing an Experimental Conservancy Establishment on the Annamullay Hills, and he was appointed to act as his "locum tenens" when Michael was invalided to England in 1854. He took so kindly to these new duties that in 1857 when Michael was again invalided and had to relinquish the

THE PILLAR ROCKS, PULNEY MOUNTAINS.

work altogether, he succeeded permanently to the appointment, and afterwards became an Assistant Conservator under Dr. Cleghorn in the forest department which sprang from this beginning. He had, however, at times to return to his military duties, and in 1860 he went with his regiment to Hong Kong, returning to Madras in February, 1861. In 1862 he was given a roving commission by Sir Charles Trevelyan to make drawings for the Government of all the hill plateaux in Southern India which were likely to suit as Sanitaria, or quarters for European troops, &c.

A series of careful drawings of the Annamullay, Pulney[1] and Shervaroy Hills was the result.

While at work on this commission he had great opportunities not only of following his favourite pursuit, but also of observing the habits of the various animals inhabiting the different districts.

These well-known drawings proved that he was a most accurate observer as well as a careful draughtsman. Each series of drawings was accompanied by a full report of the districts.[2]

The Pulney mountains are situated between 10° and 10° 15″ north latitude, and 77° 20′ and 77° 55″ east longitude, in the Madura District. They extend in a north-easterly direction from the great mass of mountains known as the Western Ghauts, to which they are connected by an Isthmus, or ridge of hills about eight miles in width; being completely isolated on every other side. To the north are the Districts of Coimbatore and Trichinopoly; those of Madura and Tanjore lie to the east; Tinnevelly and Travancore to the south and west.

There is an abundant supply of water on the higher range throughout the year. In some of the valleys, according to Captain Ward, there are extensive morasses and in the swamps near Kudaikarnal peat of very good quality has been found. On these moun-

---

[1] In the modern spelling of these mountains Pulney becomes Pulni, Annamullay—Anaimalais, Nielgherry—Nilgiri.

[2] Since these reports were sent in the Pulneys and the other ranges of hills in Southern India have been most carefully surveyed, and the population accurately taken, &c.

tains are the sources of upwards of thirty large streams which form eleven good sized rivers.

The population of the higher Pulnis consist of a mixed race viz. :—Kooroovers, Pooliars, Vadogars, Maravers, Chetties, and a few Pariahs. The Chetties are the traders, and are found in considerable numbers on the hills. The other inhabitants are occupied in cultivation, they are the dupes of the traders from the plains, from whom they purchase goods and occasionally borrow money at exorbitant interest.

Many of the inhabitants are fine robust powerful men, but they have all the appearance of being a mixed race, and there is no distinct stamp of character such as is found amongst the Todas and Kotas of the Nielgherries and the Karders of the Annamullies.

The climate of these hills appear to me to be milder and of a more even temperature than that of Ootacamund, though the altitude of the sites of the houses at Kudaikarnal is within a few feet of that of the Ootacamund Lake. There is a less amount of rain fall during the year than on the Nielgherries, but it is more equally distributed. During my stay at Kudaikarnal I kept a register of the temperature with two thermometers, one placed in the open verandah and the other in a room without a fire. The register shows a remarkable evenness of temperature.

As an instance of the salubrity of the climate, I may mention that although my servants were much exposed during the monsoon to the inclemency of the weather, yet with the exception of one case of cold and slight fever, they were perfectly healthy, which I know from experience would not have been the case at Ootacamund under similar circumstances.

In 1861 he went to the Shervaroy Hills to make a series of drawings, and the following are extracts from the report.

" The Shervaroy Hills are situated in the Salem District of the Madras Presidency, about six miles to the north of Salem, in north latitude 11° 50″ and east longitude 78° 20″. They form the northern boundary of the valley in which the town of Salem lies. Their entire length from north to south is about seventeen miles,

VIEW IN THE VALLEY OF PERUMBOOKARNAL, PULNEY MOUNTAINS.

with a breadth of from ten to twelve miles forming an irregular mass of mountains intersected by deep valleys. The superficial area of the higher plateau has been estimated at one hundred square miles, but this must include all the hills with the exception of quite the lower spurs.

The Shervaroyen on the Green Hills is the highest mountain, its elevation is variously estimated, but from 5,200 to 5,300 feet above the sea level is perhaps the nearest approximation ; the higher portions of the plateau are from 4,500 to 5,000 feet: the western and southern portions attain the greatest elevation descending to the eastward to 2,500 feet above the level of the sea. The whole range is separated into three divisions called Nàuds, *viz.*, Moch or Mogo-nàud, Salem-nàud and Mootoo-nàud. Yercaud, the present settlement, is in the latter nàud.

The inhabitants of these mountains are called Vellalers or Malayalies (mountaineers), they numbered in 1861 about 3,500 and occupy, seventy-nine villages scattered over the hills ; very little appears to be known as to their origin. According to the generally accepted tradition they emigrated from Conjeveram about six hundred years ago; in appearance and habits they differ little from the inhabitants of the plain, speaking the same language (Tamil) and being of the same religion (Hindoo). They are tolerably healthy-looking, and certainly have no appearance of a fever-stricken race. Their dress is similar to the natives of the plains ; a black cumbly is generally worn by the men in cold and inclement weather, but it appears to be considered too great a luxury for their women, who do as much, if not more, out-door labour than the male population. The Malayalies, like most other hill tribes in India, are not cleanly in their dress or habits, their villages are usually situated in the valleys amidst their cultivation, and from the peculiar shape of their huts have a very singular appearance. They are of a circular form, the walls are made of split bamboo with an outer coating of mud ; the roof is conical, and thatched with grass. .

"The Malayalies possess considerable herds of cattle and a few goats. According to Dr. Fasken's Report on the Shervaroys, written in 1824, they then appeared to have had a superior breed of *black* cattle; the distinctive color has disappeared, but the hill cattle are still superior to the ordinary run of cattle on the plains; sheep are said not to thrive on the Shervaroys and are therefore seldom met with.

"Yercaud, the principal settlement, is situated on the southern portion of the hills, or that nearest Salem, its average elevation is about 4,500 feet above the sea; the houses are scattered over irregular undulating hills. There are several good roads traversing the Settlement forming pleasant rides and drives."

"Until lately there were only two ghauts leading to the high ranges, *viz.*, the ghaut from Salem on the southern, and the Mallaporam ghaut on the northern side. The former is six miles in length; some portions of it are very steep, it might be much improved and shortened, but a road for wheeled carriages could not be made except at a great expense; by this ghaut all supplies, &c., are brought from Salem. The northern ghaut leading from the Railway Station at Mallaporam (eight miles from the foot of the hills) to Yercaud, *viâ* Nagalore, is at present an unmade bridle-path, but the gradients are easy, and it might be made into a carriage ghaut."

"A bridle-path has recently been opened down the valley leading to Athoor, a few miles to the west of Mallaporam. The Railway at this place (Athoor) approaches to within two and a half miles of the foot of the pass, the pass itself being only five and a quarter miles to the Green Hills and eight miles to Yercaud; the gradients are easy with the exception of one small portion, and a good bridle-road could be constructed at a moderate expense. The only difficulty I noticed to its being made a carriage road was the ascent of a steep spur about two and a half miles from its summit; could this be surmounted, a carriage road *viâ* Nagalore and Mallaporam would not be required. By ascending the Athoor ghaut, the summit of the Shervaroys can be reached from Madras with the greatest ease in twelve hours, an immense saving of time compared with the hitherto used route, *viâ* Salem, where the traveller had to remain one night on the plains, or if he attempted to make the ascent, seldom reached his destination

LAKE OF YERCAUD, SHERVAROY HILLS.

before midnight. This pass is the nearest approach to the Green Hills, the highest and most healthy portion of the Shervaroys where it is hoped when the unreasonable dread of fever has disappeared, the wealthy residents of Madras will eventually establish their *country villas.* Though the Green Hills are only a few hundred feet higher than Yercaud, and the difference of temperature is scarcely two degrees, yet there is a freshness in the mountain air, which is altogether lost amidst the dense vegetation of Yercaud. This change is most marked to any one leaving the latter and ascending the former place. Water is more abundant on the Green Hills than elsewhere, three or four streams, that never fail even in the driest seasons, are to be found here, as well as an extensive range of excellent soil suitable for gardens, and numerous sites for houses commanding the most extensive and grandest views on the Shervaroys. Several miles of road could be constructed without difficulty, and a lake formed in the swamp below the village of Munjaykoottay. It is difficult to conceive a more charming spot than the Green Hills might become with building plots well selected, grounds judiciously planted out, and a fine lake.

"The Casuarina grows well on the hills, and is highly ornamental. There are also several Australian acacias and eucalypti, but they have rather a stunted appearance and certainly do not thrive as well as on the Nielgherries or Pulnies. The Rhododendron is not found on the Shervaroys, it requires a greater altitude; according to Dr. Cleghorn, Conservator of Forests, it is not met with in Southern India below an elevation of 5,500 feet.

"Many fruits, both European and Indian, succeed well on these Hills, apples, pears, peaches, plums, loquats, figs, strawberries, oranges, lemons, limes, citrons, shaddocks, guavas, plantains and the Brazil cherry, are found in the gardens. The oranges are excellent, quite equal to those of Coonoor. The pear tree grows in every hedge and garden of Yercaud in great abundance; there are two kinds both of a coarse quality, but they are left in an almost wild state and might be much improved by cultivation, or others of a better description introduced. Apples appear to succeed well; but there are not many trees as yet on the hills. The loquat abounds, and some of the trees bear fruit of a very superior flavour. The vine when tended with care, has succeeded well.

"Nearly every kind of European vegetable grows to perfection, and excellent potatoes might be abundantly produced.

"The flowers that have been imported, such as geraniums, roses, fuschias, heliotrope, verbenas, &c., grow almost wild, especially the roses and geraniums.

"There can be no doubt that the Shervaroys might become the market garden of Madras, with the Railway at the foot of the hills, and the Athoor ghaut open to traffic, fruits and vegetables fresh from the gardens could be delivered in the Madras market twelve hours after leaving the hills. There is very good garden ground on the Green Hills, and an ample supply of water might be obtained by sinking wells should no stream be available. Capital laid out in establishing a large fruit and vegetable garden to supply the city of Madras would certainly prove more remunerative than Coffee planting, but it must not be expected that any garden on a large scale can be established without considerable labour, care and expense; like most rich and uncultivated land, the soil abounds with destructive grubs, caterpillars and other insects. Many persons who have attempted to form vegetable gardens have given up in despair on seeing crop after crop destroyed by insects; one especially, a dark nearly black grub is the most destructive of all, and very difficult to get rid of, but with care and perseverance the soil can be sufficiently cleaned of them and good crops produced, as a few of the gardens on the hills testify.

"The climate of the Shervaroys is exceedingly delightful, being at a much less elevation than the Nielgherries, and consequently warmer, the new arrival from the plains feels none of the bad effects from the sudden change so liable to occur on reaching the colder climate of Ootacamund; yet the air on these hills is sufficiently bracing to be invigorating, and the effect produced on the languid heat-stricken frame of a person long resident on the plains is astonishing. The temperature appears to be very even throughout the year.

"The game animals found on these hills are tigers, panthers, bears, bison, sambur, spotted-deer, muntjack, or barking-deer, mouse-deer, wild hog, jungle fowl, spurfowl, hares, partridges, quails, also woodcock and snipe in the season. The tiger is rarely met with on the higher range. Panthers are more numerous, and the planters and other residents occasionally have their dogs carried off by these prowling depredators. There are very few bison, and those only found in the lower thickly wooded valleys where bears are also occasionally met with. Sambur are not numerous; none are found on the upper ranges. The spotted-deer inhabits the bamboo jungles on the slopes of the hills, and has at rare intervals been seen in the neighbourhood of Yercaud; but it is now so reduced in number that the most persevering sportsman rarely falls in with it. The muntjack, generally known as the jungle sheep, is pretty numerous amongst the Coffee gardens and jungles of Yercaud; but from its wary habits and the jungle being so continuous and thick it cannot be easily driven, and is consequently seldom shot. Wild hog are also rather numerous, but for the same reasons are not often killed. The little mouse-deer is rarely seen, but its foot prints are found in many places. The jungle fowl, spurfowl, hares, partridges and quails, afford an occasional shot during a morning's walk, but good dogs are required to find them. There is tolerable woodcock and snipe shooting during the season from November to March.

"The Malayalies are great adepts at netting game. Even the tiger being occasionally captured by them; the mode they adopt is to enclose a large space with nets and drive the game towards them, when the animals become entangled in the meshes and are destroyed in their attempts to escape.

"The cause of these mountains not having become so frequented, as they deserve to be, is owing to the bad name they have obtained for fever. Many people at Madras would as soon encamp in the most deadly jungle as go to the Shervaroys, there is no doubt that in occasional seasons when the south-west monsoon has been late in setting in, there is a good deal of fever on the hills during the months of May and June, and at long intervals there have been severe outbreaks of fever; but few stations in India are entirely free from such outbreaks, and as a general rule the Shervaroy fever is not of a severe type and is easily amenable to treatment.

"Assistant-Surgeon W. R. Cornish, Secretary to the Principal Inspector General Medical Department, who inquired minutely into the subject during his visit in 1861, is of opinion that the Shervaroy fever, when it does occur, is quite as much under control of medicine as the same form of disease elsewhere.

"*Climate suitable for Invalids.*—It is not improbable that some forms of disease, which are aggravated by the Nielgherry climate, may be treated with benefit on the Shervaroy Hills, such as rheumatism, chronic affection of the liver, bowels, air passages, &c. It is not however to invalids suffering from organic disease that our mountain climates hold out much ground of hope; but rather to those who are simply exhausted in mind and body from prolonged exposure to a high temperature in a low country, and who need rest from work and a cooler air to breathe. These are the cases which benefit in a remarkable degree from a short residence on the Shervaroys.

"Admitting the full force of the objection that the hills are occasionally malarious, it is no less certain that they are free from many of those sources of disease which abound in the plains. Malignant cholera and dysentery destroy one-half of those who die in our European armies located on the plains, 'fevers' on the other hand, do not cause more than one-tenth of the whole mortality. There can be no question that where a choice of evils is to be had it is best to adopt the minor one. Our statistics show that the mortality from fevers, including the 'continued' and 'typhoid' varieties in the Madras Presidency, do not exceed one per cent.; whereas of every two Europeans attacked by the cholera-poison, one dies, and of every 100 cases of dysentery, seven prove fatal."

"The Shervaroy Hills have as yet enjoyed an immunity from cholera, and it is evident that with due attention to sanitation, this terrible pest can never obtain a footing. Its germs have, as before shown, been frequently introduced, but the conditions necessary to their development have as yet been wanting. Dysentery, hepatitis, and insolation, are diseases unknown amongst Europeans in the Shervaroy climate."

In 1863 he made a series of sketches on the high ranges of the Annamullies. In his report he says: "They are situated on the southern boundary of the Coimbatore District, in the Madras Presidency, and are divided into the Higher and the Lower Ranges; the latter, lying to the westward contain the famous Teak Forests; their average elevation is not more than 2,000 feet above the level of the sea, with peaks and ridges rising to 4 and 5,000 feet. The whole of the lower range, with the exception of a few bare and rocky peaks, is covered with dense forest containing much valuable timber; whereas the higher range lying to the eastward consists of extensive open grassy hills and valleys with shola forests similar to those on the Neilgherries and Pulnies, varying in elevation from 6,000 to 8,000 feet and upwards, above the sea level. The range is only separated from the Pulnies, which lie to the eastward, by the valley of Ungeenaad; this valley is not more than 12 or 15 miles across in a straight line; its western end is shut in by two blocks of well-wooded mountains with plateaux on their summits forming a connecting link between the Annamullies and the Pulnies. Viewed from the line of railway near Coimbatore, the Annamullays and Pulnies appear as one continuous range of mountains.

"The high ranges were first visited in 1851 by General Michael who was then in charge of the teak forests; during the visit he discovered the beautiful valley now bearing his name.

"The distance from the foot of the hills, *viâ* Appia Mullay to Michael's Valley, is about 20 miles, viz., 9 miles to Appia Mullay and 11 miles further on to the valley.[1]

"I was on these mountains for two months with eight Native followers who were all perfectly healthy, with the exception of two slight cases of fever, brought on by a day's exposure to cold and wet (the Natives at Ootacamund frequently contract fever from

[1] It is in this valley that a shooting camp was prepared in 1875 for H.R.H. the Prince of Wales.—ED.

similar causes), and taking into consideration the indifferent shelter afforded, their constant exposure to all the vissicitudes of climate during a period when elsewhere fever generally prevails, it may be accepted as a very fair criterion that the position of Michael's valley and the surrounding plateau is most favourable to health, and the high ranges once attained, there need be no apprehension of fever under ordinary circumstances. The Natives of these mountains do not exhibit the same symptoms of an unhealthy region, as is observed in the inhabitants of the lower Pulnies; and I think I may safely assert, that these hills will eventually prove fully as free from fever as the Nielgherries, and possessing a climate equal to any of the ranges at present known."

"It is difficult to judge the superficial area of a mountain range with accuracy by the eye, but having walked over nearly, indeed, I may say, the whole of the Annamullay Plateau, I think I am not far wrong in estimating it to be between 80 and 100 square miles, but this includes a large tract situated in the Travancore territory. The broken nature of these mountains causes the scenery to be far more varied and beautiful than generally met with either on the Pulnies or Nielgherries; but, as may be expected from their propinquity, there is much similarity in many respects in all three ranges. The general trend of the Highlands is N.N.E. and S.S.W., the highest elevations being to the north-east and to the south, gradually decreasing in sloping undulating hills towards the west, excepting the Arnee Moody mountain and its plateau; which is situated at the extreme S.S. West end of the range."

"I will now proceed to relate events attending an excursion I made to the great Arnee Moody mountain *viâ* 'Coomarikul,' the 'Kartu Mullay,' and across the two last mentioned blocks of table-land, this portion of the hills having never before been visited, that I am aware of. I first attempted to reach the mountain near the end of April, but owing to excessive inclemency of weather was obliged to return to Michael's valley. On the 4th May, I again started for the mountain, accompanied by Mr. Faulkner of the 17th Lancers. Our first march was to Coomarikul Mullay, by a path used by the

Pooliars and Moodoowars, of very easy gradients, which, as Michael remarks in his report, "might be cantered over on horse-back in its 'present state,' the distance by this path is about seven miles; between Coomarikul and Michael's valley we passed two remarkable precipices situated on each side of a wooded valley leading to the westward; these precipices must have at some remote period been sea-worn cliffs, as they could be formed in no other way. Clouds obscured the distant view, or part of the Kartu Mullay plateau would have been visible beyond the valley which trends away to the north-west. Our next encampment was at the foot of the Kartu Mullay, to reach which we had to ascend the summit of the Coomarikul Mullay, and proceed to the westward along the precipitous ridges overhanging the Ungeenaad valley. The views from this mountain are the grandest and most extensive I have ever beheld; some of the precipices are of stupendous magnitude, and the charming variety of scenery, comprising undulating grassy hills, wooded valleys, rocky crags, overhanging precipices, the green fields, in the valley of Ungeenaad, the grand mass of the Pulnies beyond, and the blue ranges in the far distance, present a view far beyond my power to describe, and which must be seen to be appreciated; in a word, the scenery in the Annamullays is surpassingly grand, and incomparably beauful; on our way to the Kartu Mullay we disturbed several herds of ibex, which, as they bounded amongst the crags and precipices, added greatly to the effect of the grand and wild features of the country we were passing through. I noticed two or three aqueducts similar to those met with on the Pulnies, probably made by the inhabitants of the Ungeenaad valley for the purpose of conveying water to their fields; others were observed on the Puddicul Mullay. This day's march over the mountain was about six miles. The Pooliars, who were sent on ahead, had constructed two comfortable huts for us; they are most expert at this work, erecting a neat and perfectly water-tight hut in a very short time; the walls and roof are made of the hill bamboo, supported by stems of small trees, and interlaced with grass and leaves; the uprights and rafters being neatly tied together with strips of bark.

"On the 7th May, we started for the great Arnee Moody mountain, leaving our camp at 10 minutes to 6 a.m., ascending over a spur of the Kartu Mullay (at the foot of which we were encamped), we then descended on to a fine undulating plateau, and after a walk of about four miles arrived at a beautifully wooded narrow valley, through which a stream, studded with Rhododendrons, was running in a south-easterly direction. This valley rises in its centre, and another stream flows exactly in the opposite direction, viz., to the north-west; the valley is at least 1,200 feet below the plateau, the descent being exceedingly steep and rugged. After crossing the stream, we struck into a well worn elephant path, ascending the opposite slope by a series of short zigzags, these were so perfect and regular that we could scarcely believe it possible they were made by those animals. After ascending the zigzags we diverged from the path leaving it on our left, and reached, by a steep ascent, a magnificent plateau considerably higher than the one we had just crossed, and apparently about 7 miles long by 4½ miles broad, being by far the most extensive table-land on the range; it is studded with sholas, and watered by two streams of considerable size, the largest winding in a northerly direction through undulating hills bordered by a broad swamp capable of being converted into an extensive lake. This stream eventually descends into the deep valley previously mentioned, forming a picturesque water-fall. The other stream rises in an extensive morass, and takes an easterly course falling into the western end of the Ungeenaad valley; besides these two large streams numerous smaller ones run into them.

"This plateau is, I believe, to be nearly if not quite as high as that of Ootacamund. The Arnee Moody itself is separated from it by a deep precipitous wooded ravine. It could only be reached by making a detour to the left or east, descending into a rather deep valley, and then ascending the left hand spur. The ascent occupied us one hour and ten minutes fast walking. Its summit is full 1,500 feet above the plateau, and consists of a narrow ridge about 300 or 400 yards in length running north-east and south-west. A range of hills extends for some distance to the west, with open grassy summits, but no table land; beyond this mountain immense forests are seen to the westward as far as the eye can reach, resembling in some measure the prospects from the hills to the west of Neddivuttum on the Neilgherries, but the forests appear far more extensive. Unfortunately the clouds soon shut out the view, preventing my completing a sketch of the plateau from the summit. This grand mountain, standing out alone as it does amongst smaller hills no doubt appears higher than it really is, but viewing it from several points, more especially on a clear day, from the Nielgherries, confirms me in the opinion that it is the most lofty on the Annamullay Range, and it may perhaps prove to be a rival even to Dodabetta, as yet considered the highest mountain south of the Himalayas; the strong resemblance it bears to the Peermarl Mullay on the Pulnies is very remarkable. The descent occupied us fifty minutes. On our return, we followed an elephant path for several miles, the gradient of this path was truly wonderful, these sagacious animals avoiding every steep or difficult ascent with the skill of engineers! We were four hours and twenty-five minutes going, and four hours and twenty minutes returning, exclusive of stoppages. We walked as fast as we could and the nature of the ground would allow, in order to reach the summit of the mountain while clear of clouds, and to avoid being benighted on our return. I think, therefore, the distance between the camp at Kartu Mullay and the great mountain cannot be less than fourteen or fifteen miles. On our return from Kartu Mullay to Michael's valley, we found a more direct route leaving Coomarikul Mullay to the east. We again struck on an elephant's path, which, like those previously fell in with, avoided every steep ascent, except at one hill which was cleverly zigzagged, owing to masses of sheet rock preventing a regular incline being taken.

"The Pooliars declared they had never been on the mountain before, and did not know its name; but they told a gentleman who visited the range subsequently, that it was called the Arnee Moody (elephant's forehead), and as such I find it is entered in the original unreduced map of the Great Trigonometrical Survey.

"The finest apparent site for a settlement is the great plateau of the Arnee Moody; but one important question to be solved is the amount of rain-fall during the monsoons; this has not yet been ascertained, though from the appearance of the sholas, the moss and lichens on the trees, &c., I am of opinion it is not much greater than that on the Pulnies and considerably less than the fall to the westward of Ootacamund. The area of this range is of such limited extent that there can hardly be any great difference in the amount of rain at one spot or another, and there is reason to suppose the whole hills would be quite habitable throughout the year. It is to be regretted that I failed to reach this part of the hills on my first attempt, for had I then succeeded, I could have remained some days in the vicinity and thoroughly explored the country, but the second excursion was so late in the season that I was obliged to hasten back to my head quarters and prepare to leave the hills before the heavy rains set in; had the Tooracadavoo river become flooded and impassable, there was no possibility of obtaining supplies from the low country.

"With the superior advantages of the Nielgherries and Pulnies, it will probably be many years before any extensive settlement is formed on the Annamullays, unless the country is opened up by roads, then the thousands of acres of land suitable for chinchona, tea, and coffee, would soon attract planters to these lovely hills.

"The only approaches to the hills that I am aware of, are— 1st, from Kotoor on the north, up the valley of the Tooracadavoo to Michael's valley; 2nd, from Dhullee or the north-east over the Appia Mullay ridge; and 3rd to ascend the hills from the south-eastern side, *viâ* the valley of Ungeenaad on to the Coomarikul plateau or the plateau beyond Kartu Mullay. I believe a road could be made for wheeled carriages up either the Tooracadavoo or the Ungeenaad valleys without any very considerable difficulties; but I question if it would be advisable to construct anything more than a bridle-path over the Appia Mullay. The advantage of this latter route is the being able to secure a safe halting place half-way up on the Appia Mullay ridge; whereas both the other roads pass through more than twenty miles of dangerously feverish country before safe halting ground can be reached.

"The Highlands are entirely uninhabited; but there are two tribes inhabiting the lower spurs of the range called Pooliars and Moodoowars. I only met with the former; both tribes cultivate to a small extent, felling, however, large tracks of valuable forest to raise their wretched crops of ragee and bullar (dholl). I particularly noticed the great extent of forest cleared for Coomri cultivation since 1858.

"The Pooliars are a wild looking race, somewhat resembling the Karders and Mulcers who inhabit the slopes more to the north and westward; but the most marked peculiarity about them, as stated in Major Michael's report, is their hair, which they allow to grow to an enormous length, tying it up in a huge knot at the back of their heads; others again, appear to take no pride whatever in their hair, allowing it to stand out in dishevelled locks, giving them a most wild and uncouth look, like the drawings I have seen of the savages of Australia. Some of the young men wear their hair in large bunches at the sides, bound round the forehead with a small brass chain, these appeared to be the *dandies* of the tribe; in many instances the hair when let down came considerably below the hips, but I did not see the man with his hair trailing on the ground described by Major Michael, he was away at a distant village. The dress of both the men and women is similar to that of the inhabitants of the plains, when they can afford it; though in general the dress of the former consisted of nothing more than a ragged waist cloth. I observed one or two men wearing turbands, and was told that they were well to do, and could afford them.

"The Pooliars have a few goats and fowls; their villages consist of scattered bamboo huts thatched with grass; those in the village of Poondy were well made, some of the houses having 'pandals' in front of them, and looked more comfortable than many of the native huts in the plains; besides the villages named above, they have several temporary hamlets. On my way up to the high ranges I passed two of these that had been burnt down by the recent annual fires, they being deserted by the occupants during the hot season. The owner of one of the hamlets was with me carrying a load, and this was the first intimation he had of the catastrophe; his store of ragee had been stowed away in chatties, and placed in one of the huts; he did not appear to care about the destruction of the huts, as they could be easily re-built; his great anxiety was to ascertain the damage done to his store of grain, and his consternation was great when he found the larger portion of it baked into a cindery cake. The Pooliars appear not to be at all particular as to what they eat; flesh of all kinds of animals is greedily devoured, and *rats* are a very favourite dish amongst them; they have a most ingenious rat-trap made of a bamboo stuck upright and bent with a string like a bow with a clever arrangement of noose and catch near the ground, and placed in front of the rat hole. They also catch jungle fowl and other birds with this spring. From their propensity to falsehood it was difficult to obtain anything reliable regarding their customs. They informed me that no man is allowed more than one wife, and can only re-marry twice; the marriage ceremony consists principally of feasting and drinking, the bride's father having to bear the principal expenses; they declared that no cases of intoxication ever occurred during these ceremonies; that a drunken man on such an occasion would be most severely beaten by the tribe; the probability being that there is not a single sober individual in the whole company as long as the drink lasts! They bury their dead, and on the third day the mourners break chatties of milk and water over the grave, after which they never revisit it. I could obtain very little information with regard to their religion; they said they performed 'pooja' to a god called Pooliar, bringing cocoanuts, honey, and flowers, and pouring milk on the idol; giving some of the honey to the Priest *and keeping some themselves!*

"I did not meet with the Moodoowars during my sojourn on the hills; they appeared to avoid me; for on the first occasion of my proceeding to Coomarikul Mullay, I found a freshly deserted encampment, which, from its appearance, they had only occupied for a short time, though by the preparations they had made it was evidently intended for a more permanent camp. According to the Pooliars' information, there are not more than fifty Moodoowars on the hills, probably only one clan visits the eastern portion of the high ranges frequented by the Pooliars. They appear to be a wandering race, cultivating small patches of ground; they possess herds of cattle and buffaloes, with which they till the soil; and when the grass is fresh and green after the annual fires they drive them on to the higher ranges to graze. They have no fixed habitations, or villages; but wander over the mountains with their cattle, erecting temporary huts, and seldom remaining more than a year at one place. They eat sambur, ibex, pig, &c., but will not touch the bison, which latter the Pooliars do not object to eat; they are a timid race, and avoid strangers; they make 'pooja' to the Pooliar idols.

"The high ranges abound in ibex; every rocky crag and mountain has its herd, but they are exceedingly wild; both the Pooliars and Moodoovars possess guns, and they have periodical hunts after the ibex, which accounts for their being so shy; their mode of operation is as follows:—before the hunt takes place they erect barriers of stout bushes at various spots along the passes frequented by the ibex. At every ten or twelve feet along the barrier there is a weak spot composed of light twigs with a running nooze of rattan surrounding it, the other end of the rattan being firmly secured to a post fixed in the ground; having made these preparations, they proceed to drive the ibex towards the barriers shooting any they can get a chance at on the way. The ibex on being driven up to the barrier rush at the weak portions of it and are caught in the noozes, from which, owing to their curved horns, they cannot possibly extricate themselves, and are quickly despatched by their pursuers. The Pooliars endeavoured to persuade me that very few ibex were captured in this way, and that it was only the Moodoowars that hunted them; but from the numerous barriers I saw, it is, I imagine, a very successful method of catching them. I was surprised to find so few sambur on the range, though it was the season of the fresh green grass, hardly a deer was to be seen. The only way I can account for it is, that the open hills being divided into blocks separated by deep precipitious and almost inaccessible ravines down which there are but few passes, the deer can be easily hemmed in, and doubtless the hill men have, in their periodical hunts, taken advantage of this and captured, or so disturbed the sambur as to cause them to desert these high lands. Bison come up at times in considerable numbers; but while I was on the hills, only a few were seen; elephants cross over from one great forest to another; but they generally travel during the night, and are therefore seldom seen. The other animals and birds found on this range are similar to those met with on the Nielgherries and Pulnies.

"It is worthy of note, that neither on the Annamullays or Pulnies is the edible wild strawberry to be found, though so common on the Nielgherries. Captain Beddome mentions that the rose is also absent on the Annamullays. I omitted to notice this; but I have met with it frequently on the Pulnies. The shola trees on both these ranges are of much larger growth than those on the Nielgherries; but whether owing to superior soil or climate, or both combined, I am unable to say. In a shola on the eastern plateau I met with a very large tree, the stem measuring twenty-one feet in circumference, five feet from the ground.

"At the time of my visit, the Natives on the plains had the greatest dread of the Annamullays, declaring that any one going to the high ranges was certain to contract the very worst kind of jungle fever. The teak forests to the westward have always had a very bad name for fever, and not without cause; but I have been told that on the estates now opening out, and referred to in this report, there has been very little fever. Should this prove to be the case, I imagine coolies in time will proceed as willingly to work in the Annamullays as they now do in Wynaad."

In March 1866 he went to the Bababooden Hills for the purpose of making drawings. "These hills," he reported, "are from 4,000 to 6,000 feet in height. (The highest peak, viz., Coller Nulley above the bungalow being 6,000 feet above the level of the sea.) They are in the shape of a horse-shoe, the two ends being nearly due west, and measuring round the curve, are between twenty-five to thirty miles in length. In the centre of the horse-shoe is the Janga Valley which, with the exception of a few patches of cultivation is dense jungle and

THE UPPER FALLS, NEAR MUDDIKULL, BABABOODEN HILLS.

said to be very unhealthy. The breadth of the horse-shoe at the curve taking it straight across is about three to four miles, and diagonally it is about fifteen miles. The hills slope away towards both ends of the shoe. Santawaree on the slopes of the Poligar Hill Fort of Camron Droog is 4,000 feet above the sea. A ghaut up which carts can travel leads from there to Collerhulty between three and four miles distant. There is also an old ghaut that zigzags up the steepest part of the slopes passing below the peak of Coller Nulley. The rhododendron does not grow here, nor the wild strawberry, but the raspberry and the Nielgherry broad leaved blackberry are abundant, and branches of the trees are loaded with moss, lichens, and orchids. It is said that frost never appears there. There are no jackals on these hills. I noticed the Blackbird (*Merula simillina*), the Yellow-billed Babbler (*Malacocircus malabaricus*), the Bulbul (*Hypsipetes nielgherriensis*), the Cinnamon or Bronze-backed Pigeon (*Carpophaga cuprea*), the Painted Bush Quail (*Perdicula erythrorynchа*), and other hill birds common to the Nielgherries and other mountain ranges. Black Eagles (*Neopus malaiensis*), Crows and Kites were plentiful, but I saw no Sparrows. There are no black monkeys, but the Grey Langur (*Presbytis priamus*) is very numerous."

"On the 16th of May, whilst exploring on the hills above Muddikal, I discovered a very fine waterfall. The upper falls are about 300 yards above the lower, but both were visible from where I was standing. In the upper falls, the water comes rushing over a precipitous rock in great volumes and falls without a break for 240 feet, then rushes through a mass of huge rocks, forming fine rapids to the lower fall, where it precipitates itself 180 feet into the valley below. I had a hot struggle over the slippery grass, and through the jungle to the upper falls, and on my way came on the body of a sambur killed by a tiger—nothing could exceed the beauty of the scene from the upper falls.

"On the 20th I left these hills without much regret, the utter failure of the rains prevented me from getting any sport, and my health was very indifferent during the whole of my sojourn. On the 25th I arrived at Belloor, remaining a day at the Bungalow so as to visit the Temple, the carving on the walls of which is perfectly wonderful and most beautfully executed; some of the dancing girls and other figures are perfect gems, and the scrolls of exquisite pattern. The brickwork door topped with metal plates, is different to any I have seen in Southern India, the carvings reminded me of those in Java; the Temple of Haliabede, which we visited the next day, is still more elaborate and even more beautiful. There are two gigantic bulls at the entrance."

In August, 1870, his health being very indifferent, he obtained three months' leave and went to Australia. He visited St. George's Sound, Melbourne, Sydney, and Adelaide, and returned to Madras in November much recruited in health. He finally left India after thirty-five years' service, on the 20th June, 1871, and arrived at Southampton on the 29th July following.

The "Oriental Sporting Magazine," in noticing his departure, has the following passage:—

"The great Sportsman and Shikarie who has recently left these "hills for England on account of failing health, is Colonel Douglas "Hamilton, than whom a truer friend, a more kindly gentleman, a "keener observer of nature, and a more enthusiastic sportsman it has "never been our good fortune to know. The regret at his departure "is universal. We may truly state that he has legitimately shot more "game on these hills than any other sportsman, and a sight of the "trophies that adorn the walls of his house, of the sketches and "incidents of the chase, and the relation thereof was a rich treat, "and one never again to be experienced."

From 1872 to 1887 he annually rented a moor and deer forest in Scotland, for the purpose of following his favourite pursuit of deer stalking, and many a grand stag has fallen to his rifle. The invigorating air of the Highlands restored his health and strength in a remarkable manner, and the way in which, after running at racing pace for some distance to intercept a stag, he would put his rifle to his shoulder, and bring him down when in full career was wonderful. His habit of shooting with a rifle when standing, used to elicit expressions of surprise from those who happened to be out with him.

I well remember an old stalker's astonishment when, after getting up to within some 90 yards of his first stag, which was lying down, instead of waiting till it rose, he jumped on the flat surface of a rock, gave a loud whistle, and as the beast bolted away dropped him on his tracks with a shot through the heart. "Well," said the old man, "I never saw the like o' that."

He never appeared to suffer from severe exertion and fatigue till the autumn of 1887, when, from constant exposure in bad weather he got a violent chill, and from that date, although at times appearing to get fairly well he never recovered his health, and early in the present year after a sharp attack of influenza, which produced great exhaustion, he suddenly passed away on the night of the 20th of January, 1892.

EDWARD HAMILTON.

Dates of Gen. Douglas Hamilton's commissions (from the Quarterly Indian Army List of 1891):—

Douglas Hamilton, M.I.

Ensign	1st	January,	1874 (evidently a misprint for 1834 the year he went to Addiscombe).
Lieutenant	12th	June,	1837, the year he arrived in Madras.
Captain	31st	January,	1838.
Major	2nd	March,	1847.
Lieut.-Col.	29th	June,	1853.
Colonel	1st	January,	1862.
Major-Gen.	1st	January,	1867.
Lieut.-Gen.	1st	October,	1877.
General	1st	December,	1888.

CONTENTS.

CHAPTER IV.

Singapore—Java—Labuan.

CHAPTER V.

Bears.

CHAPTER VI.

Ibex Shooting on the Nielgherries, Annamullies and Pulnies.

CHAPTER VII.

ELEPHANTS.

CHAPTER VIII.

TIGERS, LEOPARDS, &c.

CHAPTER IX.

CHAPTER X.

The Sambur and other Deer.

LIST OF ILLUSTRATIONS.

CHAPTER I.

CHAPTER II.

CHAPTER III.

CHAPTER IV.

CHAPTER V.

CHAPTER VI.

CHAPTER VII.

CHAPTER VIII.

CHAPTER IX.

CHAPTER X.

STALKING ANTELOPE WITH PONY.

CHAPTER I.

ANTELOPE SHOOTING.

ANTELOPES—DIFFERENT SPECIES—THEIR HABITS, ETC.—MODE OF APPROACHING ANTELOPES—SPEARING ANTELOPES—COURSING THE FAWNS—COURSING THE SWEET SCENTED FOX—TAKING THE BLACK BUCK WITH THE CHEETA—THE MOUNTAIN ANTELOPE—IS IT A DISTINCT SPECIES—THE INDIAN BUSTARD—BEST MODE OF STALKING THEM.

MY earliest introduction to big game shooting was at Kulladghee in the Bombay Presidency in 1839-40; my regiment, the 21st M.N.I., having been sent there to take the place of one which had gone to the front in the first Afghan Campaign. In those days antelopes were very numerous, but very wild and difficult to approach. There were two species—(1) the antelope of the plains, *(Antilope cervicapra = bezoartica)*, the male of which is known to sportsmen as the black buck, very graceful in its movements as it bounds over the open ground, and whose handsome head and horns are much prized as trophies.

The colour of the males (black buck) is a rich dark glossy brown (almost black in the old ones) above, the lower parts, abdomen, and inner parts of the legs, white—head, nape and back of the head a rufous yellow, nose and lips white and a large white ring round the eyes. The females are a pale yellowish fawn colour above, with a pale lateral streak from shoulders to haunch, and white beneath.

The height at the shoulder of the male is about thirty-two inches; length about four feet, not including the tail which is about seven inches. The horns vary considerably, from twenty to twenty-seven inches. In some very rare instances females have been found with horns, but as a rule they are hornless.

The second species is the Ravine antelope, Indian gazelle, or Chikára (*Gazella bennetti*), frequenting, as its name implies, the ravines and rocky hills. It is a little larger than the Egyptian gazelle, of a light chestnut colour, with the chin neck and breast white, both male and female have horns; the latter very much smaller than the male and not ringed. I used to enjoy prowling after them at early dawn; the ground was stony and noisy in many places so that it was difficult to get near the wary little beauties without the most careful stalking. This antelope is said never to drink.

When I first commenced rifle shooting I was much too eager, and used to fire very long shots, often at from five to six hundred yards, and as might be expected, generally missed; and in consequence I had to stand a considerable amount of chaff. I remember one day, being out with two of my brother officers, I took a very long shot, far too long, at a black buck. I distinctly heard the flop of the ball striking him, but they laughed at me and joked me about broken legs, hitting a stone, and other such chaff; and as the antelope "chulled" so well, I fully concluded that I had made a miss. I managed to get within shot of him again ; but I had my doubts as to the result as I thought I saw the ball strike the ground; however, he soon laid down, and then I knew he must have got it rather hot. When within a hundred yards or so he got up, and I then saw some blood on one of his forelegs. I had with me two capital dogs, Noble and Judy, crosses between the arab and the english greyhound with just enough of the poligar blood to give them courage, so I slipped them and away they went. The pace soon began to tell on the buck, and Noble seized him by the haunch, the antelope managed to throw him off, but the dog again got up to him and laid hold of his neck and pulled him over. I found that I had struck him with both my shots, the second one having gone through his lungs. I was at least two hundred and fifty yards away when I fired the first shot. The run with the dogs, before they pulled the buck down, was fully three quarters of a mile, so this time I came home *koosh*. I went on persevering, taking more pains and not firing till within a proper distance, and soon became a better and steadier shot, and the good-humoured chaff ceased.

As I have previously stated, these animals were at times so wild that it was often almost impossible to get within rifle shot. I soon found that the best mode of proceeding was by stalking them from behind my pony, making the syce move slowly on; even then it was no easy work and often required a long trudge, sometimes of many miles, before I could get within shot; I always made my syce or horse-keeper carry a hog-spear, and when I was lucky enough to cripple a black buck, I jumped on my horse and taking the spear endeavoured to ride him down, and many an exciting chase I have had after a wounded buck, which appeared to go just as fast on three legs as on four, sometimes taking me over at least seven miles before I could plant the spear into him and bowl him over.

I was one day following a herd with only one black buck in it; I took a running shot as he crossed me at a trot about a hundred yards off; the wind was blowing hard, I heard no "tell," and as the buck dashed on at speed I thought I had missed; however, I took a look at him with the telescope and saw on his flank a peculiar dark mark, and after getting closer and having another look, I could see that the dark mark was blood. I at once mounted and gave chase; for some distance he bounded along as if nothing had happened, but when he found me pressing him he left the herd and made for every bit of jungle he could find, gaining on me considerably; however I stuck to him like a leech. He was once or twice joined by other antelopes, but I knew my victim by the blood on his flank; once he laid down and when I got up to him I could not spear him on account of the bushes, and on he went again, taking me right back to the village. I ran him up the slope of a well where the bullocks work, and he had no help for it but to jump down the well or over the side of the slope; he did the latter, and I gave him his quietus with the spear in his neck, after a run of between three and four miles.

I used to have capital sport coursing the half grown fawns of this antelope; they would go very strong for a mile or two, but when overtaken were easily pulled down. But the best coursing I had was with the pretty little silver grey sweet-scented fox (*Canis bengalensis*). I call it

SPEARING ANTELOPE.

sweet-scented because it has none of the peculiar strong odour of other foxes, and is therefore never hunted; rare sport it gives, twisting, turning and doubling when at full speed, often baffling the best dogs and often suddenly disappearing into a fissure in the rock, or a burrow. In these rapid doublings it is evidently assisted by its brush, which is flourished about in a very remarkable manner.

CANIS BENGALENSIS.

I very rarely allowed my dogs to course jackals, for not only do they not give much sport, but the bite of this animal is very severe, and some dogs will not hold one after being once or twice severely mauled.

When we were quartered at Kulladghee, the officers bought a fine cheeta, or hunting leopard (*Cynælurus jubatus*). I was strongly opposed to the purchase, on account of its spoiling the antelope shooting, as although a cheeta hunt is most exciting to see for the first time, it becomes very monotonous, the runs being so much alike that after a month or two no one would care to see them; but the brute had to be sent out to get his food, and as he invariably killed the finest buck in the herd, you may fancy how he spoilt sport, besides making the antelopes so wild that it was hardly possible to get near them. He was advertised for sale for a long time, but as no one would purchase him he was eventually given away, having killed on an average about two antelopes a-week for nearly three years! Hunting with this animal has been so often described that I need not say very much about it. The cheeta is taken out on a native cart drawn by a pair of bullocks; he has a coil of rope round his loins, to which another with a slip noose is attached; this ties him to the cart when not in sight of game, but when he is going to be slipped it is held by the keeper and a leather hood which covers his eyes is slipped on to the back of his neck; by careful manœuvring the cart is brought within ninety or a hundred yards of the antelope; the cheeta then becomes very excited, and on the hood being pushed from his eyes the keeper turns his head towards the herd. The moment he sees them he quietly slips off on the opposite side of the cart, and creeps rapidly along with his chest nearly touching the ground; he thus gains ten or twenty yards before the antelope catch sight of him, when at once they are off and away. In an instant he is up, and having fixed on the finest buck in the herd, he rushes at him in a series of the most astounding bounds, so swift that the antelope, although one of the fastest of animals, appears to be waiting for him; in vain the poor frightened buck tries to keep with the herd, he is obliged to circle away from it and is generally brought round in a horseshoe course of about two or three hundred yards, and killed or lost not far from the cart. The cheeta appears to throw the whole of his energy and strength into the last few bounds, and if he does not succeed in striking his prey, although he may have missed by less than an inch, he will not go a step further, but sulkily retires to the nearest bush looking the picture of feline disappoint-

"OH, GREAT KING, DON'T BE ANGRY."

ment. The keeper hastens up and crouching, salaams to him saying, "Oh, Great King, don't be angry, you will kill the next," all the time he is working round the fierce brute, who does nothing but spit and growl at him; suddenly he whips the hood over the beast's eyes and it becomes as helpless as a lamb; then seizing him by the rope round his loins he is ignominiously bundled on to the cart amidst a string of abuse quite unfit for ears polite. If the cheeta succeeds in his last spring, he appears to strike the antelope somewhere about the hocks, knocking him down, and in an instant he has him by the throat, and flinging one paw over one of the horns, holds him till the keeper comes up and cuts the antelope's throat, catching the blood in a cup, this is given to the cheeta, who greedily laps it up, and is then hooded and put on the cart, ready for another chase.

I noticed that the cheeta never penetrated the throat of the antelope with his teeth, though the victim lay so still that it appeared to be dead. I suppose it was perfectly paralysed with fear. I do not know whether this is always the case. The keeper told me this one never bit its prey; he also said that no hunting leopard was any good for the chase unless he had killed antelope when in a wild state.

CHEETA STALKING ANTELOPE.

There is another mode of hunting with this animal namely: showing him the antelope a long way off and letting him stalk them; it is most interesting to see how well he does it, taking advantage of the grass or a bit of uneven ground, and in this way working up close to the herd; but it is often very tedious watching him, as he will lie *perdu* for a long

THE KILL.

time, if he cannot advance without being seen, and generally, from his being so close, if he does get in on the herd the run is too short to be of much interest.

I have killed many an antelope since those early days in other parts of Southern India, and I was fortunate enough when shooting on the Pulneys, to come across and shoot three does of a rather rare antelope known as the mountain antelope; and again on the 26th of November, 1863, I shot a buck of the same species near Pykara on the Neilgherries. I was out after sambur and Francis (my shikarie), proposed that I should go and post myself near Neilds shola, while the men beat along the slopes; so away I went carrying the Lang rifle in the Highland sling, the Breechloader on my arm, and the Ross in my hand; as I came above the little round shola under the rocks I saw what I took to be a jungle sheep (*Cervulus muntjac*) standing looking at me amongst the rocks on the opposite slope about 140 yards off. I hesitated whether I would try the Breechloader, but I trusted to the Ross; there was a loud tell, but a lot of dust flew up, and when I got to the place, I found the bullet flattened against a rock, and it did not look as if it had gone through the animal. I took up the track and immediately found a few specks of blood which increased as I went on, and about a hundred yards further on I found the animal lying dead, it having rolled part of the way down the hill side. What was my astonishment and pleasure on finding that I had shot a buck mountain antelope. It resembles very much the does I had previously killed only the lower jaw is whiter; the lachrymal sinus was much swollen and full of white gluey matter; the horns were set at slightly different angles and their points as sharp as needles.

There has been much difference of opinion amongst Indian naturalists and sportsmen as to this animal, whether it is merely a variety of the four-horned antelope, (*Tetraceros quadricornis*) or whether it is a distinct species. Jerdon at one time considered it distinct from the northern animal, as all the specimens he procured from the Eastern Ghauts had only a vestige of anterior horns and were very pale coloured; but in deference to Mr. Blyth's matured opinion, he has followed

THE MOUNTAIN ANTELOPE.

him and united the two into one species. McMaster in his notes on Jerdon's book, considers the mountain antelope of Madras sportsmen to be a distinct species and calls it Elliot's antelope. Hawkeye states that: "the mountain antelope is but little known, and perhaps has not been heard of by many, as one of the game animals frequenting the mountain ranges of Southern India," and says "that on the Pulneys this antelope is not so scarce as it is on the Neilgherries. On those mountains which are so open and undulating, like the downs in England, with little or no woods or sholahs scattered here and there as on the Neilgherries, the mountain antelope is on ground suitable to its habits, but being swift of foot and keenly alive to danger, not easily perceived when lying in the grassy hollows, and fleeing away at the least alarm, it requires much patience and woodcraft on the part of the stalker to ensure success. This animal has all the appearance of a doe antelope of the plains in colour, size, and general features, but the colour is more sandy or very light rufous, and the hair longer and coarser than the antelope of the plains, the throat white and the same colour extending along the under parts. The fetlocks are furnished with tufts of hair, and have a *bar of white across the front* similar to that of the Nilgai, the ears are much broader than the common antelope, and have tufts of longish hair in the orifice. The horns are smooth, tapering, and exceedingly sharp at the points, about four inches in length and slightly curved forward, only found on the males; the tail between six and seven inches long. The size of the animal about the same as *Gazella bennetti*." McMaster says: "having obtained the head of one of these antelopes killed at Hassanoor in Southern Mysore, I applied to the best authority I could think of, viz., Colonel Douglas Hamilton, who had I knew a specimen of the mountain antelope, which he had killed at Pykara on the Neilgherries, and who is probably the most accomplished sportsman in the Madras Presidency. I forwarded at the same time to Colonel D. Hamilton the head. His reply is as follows, the latter part refers to the horns of both his specimen and mine, sloping from the skull at different angles to each other. "I think from the description this must be Elliot's antelope, it is evidently the same animal as mine. The only doubt is that in my specimen there is not a sign of 'spurious horns,' though it has the 'osseous bumps' which are so conspicuous in yours, but certainly are not to be 'easily detached' as stated in Elliot's description. In all other respects the measurements and description correspond exactly; though it is strange Elliot did not notice the peculiar white lower jaw which is so marked in my specimen: this and the entire absence of spurious horns may fix it as a different species. Here are my measurements, taken when the animal was fresh killed. You will see how close they are to Elliot's.

Height at shoulder	25 inches
Ditto at rump	27 inches
Length of leg	1 foot, 5 inches
Chest to rump	2 feet 2 inches
Neck	$6\frac{3}{4}$ inches
Tail	$9\frac{3}{4}$ inches
Horns	$3\frac{3}{4}$ inches

I see your horns are at slightly different angles but not so marked as mine. They are $\frac{1}{4}$ of an inch longer."

In respect to this supposed species, Mr. W. T. Blandford, F.R.S., ("Fauna of British India," p. 520,) under *Tetraceros quadricornis*' Varieties, says: "In the Madras Presidency the anterior horns are said to be rarely developed, and certainly fully adult animals occur without any, and with only small projections on the skull, but I can see no other difference; the skulls, whether the anterior horns are developed or not, are precisely similar in form and scarcely differ in size. In the case of a male that I obtained young in Nimar and that was kept alive by a friend in Bombay, the anterior horns did not appear till the third year, although the posterior horns were well developed early in the second. Doubtless many of the two-horned individuals seen are young. Blyth came to the conclusion that the two-horned form is merely a variety, and after reading all that has been written by McMaster and Sterndale on the subject, I agree with him."

The Indian bustard[1] (*Eupodotis edwardsii*) was occasionally met with on the plains and afforded good sport for the rifle; I used to stalk them in the same way as I did the antelope, with this difference, that they generally stood and allowed me to circle round them, gradually decreasing the circumference until I got within shot; their power of concealing themselves behind a small bush or tuft of grass was wonderful. They differ considerably both in colour and appearance from the European bustard, and are from four to five feet in length; generally weigh about twenty-six to twenty-eight pounds, get on the wing very easily, and fly very long distances. Jerdon states that one sportsman has killed over a thousand of these birds with the rifle. The females and poults are fair eating.

[1] See plate "Spearing Antelope," page 5.

CHAPTER II.

WOLVES—HUNTING IN CONCERT—MODE OF ATTACK—THEIR PERSEVERANCE—SELDOM ATTACK HUMAN BEINGS—JOIN GREYHOUNDS IN CHASE—SUPERSTITION AS TO THEIR BLOOD—WILD DOGS—GREAT POACHERS—HUNTING IN PACKS—ATTACKS ON THE SAMBUR—MUNGOOSE AND COBRA—MODE OF ATTACKING THE COBRA—ITS RAPID MOVEMENTS CAUSE OF SAFETY—PROTECTION FROM SNAKES WHEN OUT SHOOTING—PIG-STICKING—THE "DEAL-TABLE" HUNT AT AHMED NUGGER—MY FIRST SPEAR—TWO METHODS OF PIG-STICKING—A BOLD BOAR—SUPERIORITY OF THE ARAB HORSE—A LONG RIDE—THE HAPPY VALLEY—SMALL GAME SHOOTING.

WOLVES.

I OFTEN came across wolves when out after antelope, and on other occasions. They are generally seen in small packs of four or five, but at times in greater numbers. It is wonderful how they work in concert; on one occasion when returning with a friend from a trip to the Caves of Ellora, we saw a herd of antelope near a range of low rocky hills, and as there was a dry nullah or watercourse giving an easy approach, we decided on stalking them. While creeping up the nullah we noticed two animals coming across the plains on our left; at first I took them for leopards, but as they came nearer I saw they were wolves, and when they were about five hundred yards from the antelope they quietly laid down. After about ten minutes or so, the smaller of the two got up and trotted off to the rocky hills, and suddenly appeared on

WOLVES WATCHING ANTELOPE.

the ridge, running backwards and forwards like a scotch collie dog. The larger wolf, as soon as he saw that the antelope were fully occupied in watching his companion, got up and came as hard as he could gallop to the nullah; unfortunately he caught sight of us and bolted, and his companion seeing something was wrong, did the same. Now it is evident that these two wolves had regularly planned this attack; one was to occupy the attention of the antelope while the other was to steal up the watercourse and dash into the midst of them. How did they communicate this to each other? A problem in the history of animal life yet to be solved.

At another time a brother officer of mine was stalking a herd of antelope which were feeding down a grassy valley, when suddenly a wolf got up before him, then another and another, until fourteen wolves rose out of the grass. They were extended right across the valley in the shape of a fishing net or jelly bag, as he described it, and were lying down wind, so that as soon as the herd had got well into the "jelly bag," they would have rushed on the antelope and some must have fallen victims to their plan of attack. I once came upon a pack of wolves apparently holding a council of war; after lolling about for some time they all rose up, and separated, to all appearance having arranged their plans for the day.

The perseverance of the wolf to attain its end is also very remarkable. One day when out hog hunting I saw a wolf following an antelope with a fawn at its heels; it did not attempt to approach them, but merely kept them in view. This was early in the forenoon, and as we returned late in the afternoon near the same ground, there was the antelope and its fawn, and the wolf still following and watching them. The late Mr. B., of the Madras Civil Service, a noted sportsman and a famous shot, told me that on one occasion he was riding through some low jungle when he heard a peculiar thumping noise a little way off the road, and dismounting he stole into the jungle, taking his rifle with him; on arriving at an open space he saw a sambur hind with a small calf standing in the middle of it looking intently at a big bush, out of which rushed a large wolf and made a dash at the calf; he was instantly knocked head over heels by the hind, and at once retreated into the bush; again and again he sallied forth only to be knocked over again and again by the brave old hind; still he persevered until at last B., seeing that the deer was becoming exhausted, shot the brute the next time it came out.

Wolves used occasionally to visit our cantonment at night and many a dhobie's (washerman's) donkey, left out to forage for itself in the officer's gardens, fell a victim to these hungry marauders. One night they attacked a charger belonging to our adjutant and injured the poor animal so severely before it was rescued, that it had to be shot. It is said that native children have been carried off by wolves, but as a rule they do not attack human beings. I once came unexpectedly close upon four wolves; they showed their teeth and looked uncommonly vicious, but turned tail before I could get a fair shot at them. That they are extremely cunning as well as sagacious, and up to all kinds of dodges to circumvent their prey, there cannot be a doubt. Hawkeye (my brother, the late Gen. Richard Hamilton, C.B.), in his book on Indian Game, says:—

"Travelling along the road to the Bellarungums, I came

upon some antelope near the roadside. Following them they led me to a fine open piece of ground of two or three miles in extent, on which, and not very far apart, I saw some half dozen bustards, nine or ten wolves, and a very large herd of antelope besides those I had followed. The wolves were, I am sure, up to some dodge, for it was not until I had fired three or four shots at the bustards (missing every one) that I became aware of their presence and they then showed in pairs, at intervals of some distance and were evidently waiting their opportunity at the antelope. I lean to the idea that the wolves hold themselves in relays, each giving the antelope a burst at their utmost speed, and it is well known that the antelope when thus the pressure is kept up gets soon blown."

The same author states that a wolf once joined in the chase after an antelope with two of his dogs, and not only pulled it down but half devoured it before he reached the spot. He also states that he once saw two wolves trotting along parallel with a herd of antelope, one of the two carrying a good sized fawn in its mouth.

Captain Jackson, of the Nizam's service, told me a rather amusing story about a wolf. He was out after foxes, when he put up a young fawn, at which he at once slipped his dogs; they ran it for about a mile and a-half, when suddenly up got a wolf just in front of the dogs and joined in the chase after the antelope, and being quite fresh soon rolled it over, and the next moment there were the dogs, wolf and antelope, all of a heap, fighting and struggling. Jackson jumped off his horse, whipped off the dogs and the wolf, and secured the fawn, which appeared not to be in the least hurt. The wolf immediately sat down and began to howl at the loss of his prey and in a few moments made a dash at Jackson;

but when within a few yards he thought better of it and turned back and recommenced his howling, which brought up another wolf to his assistance, and both howled and looked extremely savage and seemed very much inclined to make another dash after the antelope; but the horsekeepers just then came up and the wolves bolted.

The natives believe that if the blood of a wolf is shed on any cultivated land, that land becomes barren.

Our Indian wolf (*Canis pallipes*) is a distinct species from the European wolf, being somewhat smaller, the height at shoulder about 26 inches; length of head and body 37 inches; tail 17 inches. It is of a hoary rufus or dirty reddish white with some of the hairs tipped with black. Tail thin and bushy, slightly black tipped; ears rather small. Blandford says that the fur is short with little or no woolly underlying fur.

WILD DOGS.

Wild dogs have decreased considerably in the last few years, but I occasionally came across them in my rambles. When they do appear, they become a regular pest to the sportsman as well as to the natives, as they drive away all the deer from the district; the sambur has a most intense dread of these poaching rascals and will leave a locality for months after being hunted by them. The first I killed was in 1855, when shooting on the Annamullies. Half way between Peramba Colum and Takady, I saw an animal cross the path which I thought was a leopard. I looked keenly into the jungle, and in the grass some eighty or ninety paces off saw something red, it looked so large that I thought it must be a tiger's head, so took a very steady aim. At the report up jumped three jungle dogs, and one went away as if hit but I could find no blood. I followed in the direction they had gone and saw one of them walking slowly up the slope of the hill in front, he stood on seeing me and I bowled him over with the left barrel. He had got a wound all along his back, some days old, seven inches long, which had opened out two or three inches wide, it was evidently a gore from a

WILD DOGS (Cuon rutilans).

deer's antler. On measuring him, I found he was exactly 4 feet from nose to tip of tail. The tail exactly 1 foot; he stood 21 inches at the shoulder; a fine strong wiry looking brute, evidently made for speed and endurance, with great length of body and very powerful loins. I only took his brush which was as thick and bushy as that of an English fox, with the tip black; he was to all appearance a very old dog.

Another time when out looking for deer I saw some animals come tearing over the opposite hill above a small detached wood; with my glass I saw a three parts grown sambur being chased by five wild dogs; they were spread out like a fan so that the outer dogs could cut off the deer in case it turned, but it got into the shola; and some time after when it broke on the other side, only three dogs came out after it, the deer having gained a considerable start, got clean away. I went down to some rocks below in hopes of falling in with these poachers, but failed to find them.

Hawkeye, in writing about these animals, says that in former days they were met with in formidable numbers, and he remembers seeing a very large pack headed by two dogs apparently much larger than the others, sweeping across near the end of the Ootacamund lake where Col. Wood's house now stands, evidently in pursuit of game. Their mode of hunting has been observed on several occasions. Ever on the move and prowling about the woods and ravines where sambur are usually found they start their game; their first object being to drive it away from the sholahs (small woods) in rushing through which the deer have the advantage as the pack cannot act in concert, and are unable to press their quarry to full speed. But once in the open they exert their wonderful powers of speed, perseverance, and endurance, driving the sambur headlong down the steeps over the hills, and generally forcing the animal to take soil when it falls an easy prey, unless a deep pool is available in which the deer is often able to keep the pack at bay.

"When at the Avalanche a few months back, I was one morning panting up that terribly steep hill behind the bungalow, I met a hind and fawn bustling down the side of the hill, in a desperate hurry with all their hair standing on end; and yet as I was to leeward and there was nothing to alarm them that I could see, I was puzzled at their behaviour; but the cause was not far off, for on reaching the point from which they had come I met three wild dogs in chase, and I am sorry to add, made a disgraceful miss at the biggest of the lot."

In the low country where there is more cover and game is plentiful, wild dogs are more abundant. In their rushes at the deer, they always appear to attack it at the flank and endeavour to disembowel it, and thus soon despatch their victim.

Jerdon's description is as follows:—General colour bright rusty red or rufus fawn colour, paler beneath; ears erect, rather large, somewhat rounded at the tip; tail moderately brushed, reaching to the heels, usually tipped blackish; limbs strong; body lengthened. Length of head and body 32-36 inches, tail about 16 inches, height 17-20 inches.

MUNGOOSE AND COBRA.

One of our officers had a tame mungoose;[1] a charming little pet; whenever we could procure a cobra, and we had many opportunities, we used to turn it out into an empty store room, which had a window some height from the ground, so that it was perfectly safe to stand there and look on. The cobra when dropped from the bag or basket would wriggle into one of the corners of the room and there coil himself up. The mungoose showed the greatest excitement

[1] *Herpestes mungo.* The Common Indian Mungoose.

on being brought to the window, and the moment he was let loose would eagerly jump down into the room, when his behaviour became very curious and interesting; he would instantly see where the snake was, and rounding his back and making every hair of his body stand out at right angles (which caused him to appear half as large again as he really was) he would approach the cobra on tip toe making a peculiar humming kind of noise. The snake in the meantime would shew signs of great anxiety, and I fancy fear, erecting

MUNGOOSE AND COBRA.

his head and hood and ready to strike when his enemy came near enough. The mungoose kept running backwards and forwards in front of the snake gradually getting to within, what appeared to us, striking distance. The snake would strike at him repeatedly and *appeared* to hit him, but the mungoose continued his comic dance apparently quite unconcerned. Suddenly, and with a movement so rapid that the eye could not follow it, he would pin the cobra by the back of the head. One would hear the sharp teeth crunch into the snake's skull, and all was over, the mungoose eating the snake's head and part of his body with seemingly great gusto. Our little favourite killed a great many cobras, and I think never was bitten. I believe the story of the mungoose eating some herb when bitten to be quite a myth, and that if really struck by the cobra it would die. I believe also that its safety consists in the perfect judgment of the distance the snake can strike. The increase of its apparent size from all his hairs standing out at right angles deceiving the snake, so that the fangs never really touch the body of the mungoose but only the hair.

People in England often ask "how about snakes when you are out beating for game?" as if the country was overrun with them. They are certainly met with occasionally, but many of them are harmless. It is surprising how few one does see, and as the sportsman nearly always wears high gaiters to protect him from the thorns and spear grass, he is quite safe from venomous snakes, as they always strike downwards, and it must be a very large snake to be able to strike a man above the knee.

HOG-HUNTING.

I saw very little of what I consider to be the finest sport in the world. I mean hog-hunting, or as it is commonly called pig-sticking. What a pity such a noble sport should be known by such an ignoble title.

The only hog-hunting I had was at Ahmed-nugger, Satara and Kulladghee. At that time I could only afford to keep one horse as a hunter and in the rough rocky ground a horse was often put "hors de combat." Still I managed to see enough to make me fully appreciate the sport.

The "Deal table hunt" of Ahmed-nugger was famous throughout India in those days; men came from all parts to join in it. The anticipation of one of those glorious meets became, as the old song has it,

> "My morning thought, my midnight dream,
> My hope throughout the day."

I shall never forget the excitement of my first spear; the hog was a small one, but from the enthusiastic expressions in my journal one would fancy it was one of the finest boars ever slain! There are two methods of pig-sticking. The Bengalees use a short jobbing spear loaded at the butt and the rider strikes almost down on the boar. In Madras and Bombay a bamboo spear between eight and nine feet in length is the weapon, and you ride at the boar with your lance in rest, as it were, but an old hog-hunter once said to me "Don't attempt to poke your spear at the boar, you must hold it free and firm, *and spear him with your spurs!* i.e., ride on to him holding your spear perfectly steady.

I once lost a splendid old boar by trying to prod him, it looked so easy.

It happened in this way; we had heard of a number of hog, and after some beating found a sow, a lot of squeakers and a boar, but they kept running from one field to another, the boar knocking over one or two beaters; at last he came out close to me (upsetting a little boy in beautiful style, luckily without hurting him), and I followed him through a narrow strip of grain leading to the open without pressing him, which if done generally makes a hog double back, and I soon got him fairly in the midaun, when at him I went, my horse, "Old Duck," behaving beautifully, and I soon had the boar within reach of my spear. I was determined this time to get my horse's head alongside of him before I made my effort, but, eager fool that I was, instead of letting the spear glide into him I made a poke, and the point not being depressed enough jerked up, and passed harmlessly over the boar's back. I made another vain attempt but the opportunity was lost, he passed into some thick grain, where the ground was heavy, and my horse being blown he gradually got ahead. I viewed him twice afterwards but he was too far off, besides he had

RATHER A STOPPER.

got to water, and it is curious how even one roll in the water will refreshen a hog; the moment before he may appear hardly able to drag his weary limbs along, one splash, and he will become as fresh as ever and go for miles. Whenever a boar finds himself pressed he at once makes for water, and therefore it is necessary to spear him if possible before he attains his object.

Some of the ground at Aḥmed-nugger was very difficult to ride over. To ascend to the crest of a rocky range of hills and ride down the steep side covered with large boulders, required a steady hand and nerve. I have seen a man ride his horse down the side of a nullah so steep that he would have been unable to get him up without the greatest difficulty; however, the Arab horse is wonderfully surefooted, and if you keep his head straight he will hardly ever fall, as he throws his hind legs under him if he trips with his fore. I have known the skin to be taken off the hocks after a ride down one of these hills. When the boar has been driven into the plain below, it is often worse riding than on the hill-side, as there are hidden holes and fissures and deep dry nullahs or watercourses to get across, as the boar generally selects the most difficult ground he can find. The beauty of hog-hunting is that you are hound and huntsman combined, added to which there is the intense excitement and the glorious uncertainty of racing for the first spear, for the boar will turn and twist so that any one well to the front has a chance. Then, when the spear is held up showing first blood, you have to fight the boldest, pluckiest animal I know. I once saw a boar receive eight spears in succession, charging each time like a knight at a tournament, and in one of these charges he actually forced himself up the spear and got to the horse's flank. I rushed to the rescue, when he turned on me, and after receiving my spear, which went clean through him and was left in him, he sat down ready to charge the next horseman that came up.

It is very dangerous leaving a spear in a boar, but sometimes it cannot be helped. We fully expected to find the horse he had attacked badly ripped, but to our surprise he was unharmed. On examining the dead boar we found he had a broken tusk on that side—a lucky escape! The rip of a boar's tusk is like the cut of a razor. I once saw a fine

Arab horse standing with one foot forward; there was nothing to be seen till the rider passed his hand down the back sinew, when he opened the lips of a large gash exactly as if a razor had been passed across the horse's leg. A boar never appears to lose his head, but always has his wits about him, and when he has made up his mind to charge, nothing will stop him.

There are some horses which will never close with a boar, they will race with the other horses, but just as the rider thinks he is going to win the first spear, they sheer off and nothing will induce them to approach the boar again. The Arab horses are the best as a rule, as they thoroughly enjoy the sport and become almost as excited as their riders. I had an Arab that would twist and turn after a wild boar like a greyhound after a hare. A shying horse out hog-hunting is enough to try the patience of Job.

In the days I am writing about, there were no railways or telegraphs and very few roads, so that if we wanted to get to any place quickly we were obliged to ask friends to post horses for us at stages of from ten to twelve miles apart. I once rode a hundred and thirty miles on a stretch to join a hog-hunting party, was out hog-hunting all the week, and then had to ride back again. I lost my way going there and had to sleep out in a field for half the night. I do not think I ever suffered so much from thirst as I did on that occasion. I was benighted, and had to go some ten or twelve miles with a couple of guides to where one of the horses was posted; there was no water on the way, and I was in a perfect agony of thirst; I suddenly heard a frog croak; in an instant I was off my pony and rushed to the spot; the guides shouted that the water was not fit to drink, but nothing could stop me, I was mad with thirst; the kind of pea soup composition I felt I was swallowing must have been very bad and it is a wonder I escaped cholera; fortunately I was young and healthy and no harm came of it.

Riding down the fearfully steep rocky hills when hog-hunting at Ahmed-nugger made us young fellows rather reckless; I once nearly paid very dear for my rashness. I was out with a brother officer at a lovely spot within a ride of the station, called the Happy Valley. The pass down to the plains was exceedingly steep and dangerous, in fact, nothing more than a foot path, very narrow in places, and very precipitous, and no one had ever ridden down it. My friend proposed we should make the attempt, so we started, I on a horse with only one eye, and unfortunately the good eye was towards the hill. On coming round a sharp turning in a very precipitous part of the pass, there was a stone painted white, a sort of "swamy" or sacred stone. My horse shied at it, and as he wheeled round with his good eye he saw the yawning gulf below. By a desperate effort he threw himself back on the path with his hind quarters dangling over the drop. I felt him gradually slipping back; fortunately there was the branch of a tree overhanging us, and by standing up in my stirrups I managed to reach it. The horse, relieved of my weight, struggled back on to the path, and I, with the assistance of the branch, did the same. It all occurred in less than a minute. I was too occupied to see how awful it was, but my friend, who was leading, told me it was one of the most frightful scenes he had ever beheld. We quietly returned to the bungalow, and never again attempted to ride down the pass of the Happy Valley.

I had more small game shooting in these days, than I ever had afterwards. We generally took a line through the low jungle with a dozen or so of beaters and shot everything in the shape of game we came across, consisting chiefly of partridges, quail, hares, florikin, with an occasional peafowl, and more rarely a chickára or ravine antelope. I have had many a pleasant day's shooting in this style, and though our bags were not great, there was a sufficient variety to keep up the excitement. A florikin, like a woodcock in England, was a prize worth getting, and many a mile I have ridden for the chance of one, when news has been brought in of their whereabouts; it is generally found in long grass, also in grassy bush jungle, flies heavily and easily shot, but eagerness to bag often results in a miss. It is a very delicate bird for the table. In some of the grass ground quails were very numerous, affording capital sport, twenty or thirty brace to one gun being not an uncommon occurrence.

We also had good duck shooting in the Indian corn stubbles; these stubbles were peculiar, the grain was planted on the margin of tanks or artificial lakes so common in India; when the periodical rains set in before the grain was ripe the fields became flooded, and on the grain ripening the cultivators cut off the corn heads, leaving the high stalks. Duck and snipe collect in these fields and afford first rate sport.

THE LESSER FLORIKIN (Sypheotides auritus).

THE BENGAL FLORIKIN (Sypheotides bengalensis).

THE BUNGALOW, DANDILLY FOREST.

CHAPTER III.

SPORTING TRIP TO THE DANDILLY FOREST, 1844.

HOPES OF SPORT—A NOVICE'S INEXPERIENCE—AMERICAN AND BEAR—DIFFICULTY OF KEEPING THE TRACK—OF SEEING ANIMALS—HINTS ABOUT STALKING—OLD EMAM THE AFRICAN—KILLING MY FIRST BISON—AFTER TIGERS—TIGER CARRYING OFF THE OFFICER—THE LUCKY GRIFFIN—OUR FIRST KILL—NO RESULT—AN UNEXPECTED MEETING—WATSON AND THE TIGER—CHASED BY HILL PONIES.

SEVENTY-EIGHT miles from Kulladghee is the cantonment of Dharwar, and about thirty-four miles beyond, on the Western Ghauts is the Dandilly Forest, where there used to be a good shooting bungalow pleasantly situated on the banks of the Kala-nuddi or Black river. We heard such stirring accounts of the sport to be had there, that I longed to get amongst the big game and forest shooting. I pictured myself killing the largest bison and the finest antlered stags, and possibly a tiger, to say nothing of leopards and bears! If hope tells a flattering tale, anticipation tells a far more flattering one; but what a falling off there is in the reality! what disappointment! The fact is, it requires a long apprenticeship to learn wood-craft. In the first place, it is not easy for a beginner always to see the game before him, which appears to an old hand to be perfectly plain; it also takes a long apprenticeship to be able to tell at a glance in what position the animal is standing, whether facing you, broad side on, or at an angle; and it is as likely as not that the bullet strikes in the wrong place. An American once said to me, "There is a mighty difference, sir, in shooting a grizzly bar [bear], and a painter [panther]; a bar stands up on his hind legs, and you looks at him and sees where his heart is, and you plugs it, but a painter, sir, you no sooner knocks the life out of one part of his body, than it runs into the t'other." Now in forest shooting a beginner looks and looks and does *not* see where the heart is, and the number of animals which get away wounded is chiefly due to this cause. Another thing which astonishes the novice is the wonderful way in which a native shikarie will track game, when to all appearance there are no indications for him to act upon. In later years, though I could never equal the natives, I could track with considerable success. I remember once taking a friend out after bison; we came on the spohr of a herd which appeared to me almost as plain as a cattle track, and after following it for some time, much to my surprise my companion said "Oh let's go home, there is nothing to be got here." It was difficult to persuade him that we were on the track of a herd of bison, and I suspect it was only when I pointed out the bull to him (which he had the good fortune to kill) that he was quite convinced I was telling the truth. There is also the difficulty of distinguishing animals on account of the adaptation of their colour to that of surrounding objects; even old hands are often deceived. For example, the axis, or spotted deer as it is generally called, is something like the fallow deer in colour, only the white spots and markings are more distinct, and the body is a brighter red; one would imagine such a conspicuous animal could be easily distinguished in the forest, but the spots and colour so amalgamate with the broken lights and shades that I have often taken a shot at what I thought was a solitary spotted deer, and have been astonished to see ten or twelve dash away. The tiger, again, with his bright body, black stripes and white markings, is most difficult to see in the forest, and even on the open hill side; at 300 or 400 yards distant not a stripe is distinguishable. More than once I have mistaken a tiger for a light-coloured hind sambur, until I have brought the telescope to bear and seen my mistake.

I had a long time to wait before I could get leave to visit this glorious forest; at last the happy day arrived, and I having procured a month's leave started with a brother officer at half-past four one fine morning, and rode as hard as we could gallop to Dharwar, seventy-eight miles distant. I had six horses posted and my companion five; there was nothing but a kind of bridle path between the two stations in those days, and although the country was very flat and open we managed to lose our way, fortunately, however, recovering it without much loss of time. The next day we rode twenty-four miles, and the following morning soon got over the remaining ten to the Dandilly bungalow. There we found old Emam, the head shikarie, waiting for us; he was quite a character and a splendid stalker—a huge stout negro considerably over six feet in height and decidedly fleshy. He was my first instructor in wood craft, and many a wrinkle he gave me, two of which I found particularly useful in after days. One was with regard to stalking a deer in the forest; to remain perfectly motionless the moment a deer catches sight of you, as the least movement will send the animal away; it may be necessary to stand thus for five or even ten minutes, but if you do not move the deer will commence feeding again; you can then approach nearer, doing so with the greatest caution, but the instant the deer raises its head you must be exactly in the same position you were when it first saw you; again you may have to wait, but each time if you have not been seen to move, the animal will gain more confidence. A curious thing is that it does not appear to be aware that you have reduced the distance by a hundred or two hundred yards; I have made many successful stalks with different kinds of animals in this way, not only in the forests but even on the open hills; it requires, however, a deal of patience and considerable quickness of sight. The other advice was, when shooting tigers on foot never to fire at one if you can possibly avoid it, when the line of the tiger's body is towards you; for when hit, if you have not succeeded in crippling him, the tiger will invariably spring forward in the line of its body; but if the body is away from you, and the tiger even looking at you, it will still spring straight forward at the shot. The only time I tried it the tiger was looking back at me about fifteen or twenty yards off, and though very slightly grazed by the bullet, it bounded straight away from me, enabling me to kill it with my second barrel.

Old Emam was a little too fond of arrack, but an excellent shikarie for all that. It was strange to meet with a negro in the wilds of this forest, but I was told there were several villages in this neighbourhood inhabited by descendants of Africans, supposed to be fugitive slaves and deserters from the hosts that formerly invaded southern India. Emam had all the appearance of a pure negro or seedee, like the coal stokers you meet with in the P. and O. steamers. Besides Emam, we hired another man, Modeen by name, who had a deal to learn to be as perfect as the old man; however he was not a bad young fellow. I killed my first bison with him; it was a fine young bull with pretty horns, but nothing to what I killed in after years, though the grand expressions I make use of in my journal, such as "bleeding monster" and so on, show how proud I was at the time of bagging him. He required several shots, and I dropped him dead when he was about to charge. I also killed my first sambur stag on this trip, a poor "beastie" as they would say in the Highlands, but I evidently did not think so at the time.

We only remained ten days in the forest as our great ambition was to get a tiger, and our best chance of doing so was in the ravines and jungles beyond the Dandilly forest. We had fair sport during the ten days, and I enjoyed the stalking immensely, especially when I had old Emam with me.

A curious incident occurred one day when I was out with Modeen. We struck the fresh track of a bull bison, followed it up, and came to where he had entered a patch of grass of some extent, and about six feet high. We stood on the edge for a minute or two peering in, when about fifteen yards from us I saw the grass twitching from side to side, very much as I should think it would do if a tiger was whisking his tail before he made up his mind to spring; I kept my eye on the spot and the rifle ready in case it should be "the gentleman in stripes." We looked and looked but could see nothing. At last Modeen took up a piece of earth and threw it at the spot; still the grass moved as before. Again he

"I JUST SAW HIS HEAD AND HORNS."

threw, but the grass continued moving. I asked what it could be. He said it must be birds, but I fancied birds would fly away! We then cautiously approached to within five yards; still we could see nothing. Again Modeen threw; the movement of the grass stopped, and I felt certain I could hear the breathing of some animal. I looked in and could see something dark in the grass, but a fallen tree being close by, it might perhaps be one of the branches. The grass began moving again; I pointed it out to Modeen; he again said it was nothing, and taking up a large bit of wood let drive straight at the spot, when instantly a huge bull bison sprang up and rapidly disappeared before I could bring my rifle to the shoulder! I just saw his head and horns as he rose; they

"EMAM TOOK UP THE TRACK."

appeared to be very large. Vexed with my bad luck; I turned home, wishing I had had old Emam with me instead of only this young half-fledged shikarie.

Another day I had a little excitement when out with Emam; we came to a place where a tiger had been dragging some animal, which, from the bits of skin and hair, we found to be a sambur. Emam took up the track with the eagerness of an old hound finding a scent, and whispered to me that we should come on the tiger directly, and that I was to shoot him "bey shuk" (without doubt). I did not half like the idea of meeting my first tiger on foot, especially as I had missed, failed to bag, is a pleasanter way of putting it, a fine bull bison that very morning! From after experience I am sure beginners often miss large game from firing through bamboos and bushes, as it is surprising how small a twig will turn a bullet quite wide of the mark; this, and what I have already written with regard to seeing where the heart is, I hope accounts for some desperate misses I have made at bison almost as big as barn doors! But to return to the tiger. I was determined that the old savage should not see that I did not like it, so on I went, cautiously creeping after him, hoping all the time that the tiger had choked himself, or had finished his dinner and made himself scarce. As luck would have it, he had done the latter, and it was on this occasion that I spoke to Emam about shooting a tiger on foot in an open forest like the Dandilly, and he then gave me the advice already mentioned; he also added that if we had come on the tiger, and he was facing us, he would not have let me fire.

On leaving the Dandilly forest we went to different places where tigers were known to be. The plan adopted was to post bullocks in likely places, and obtain, if we could, "a kill" when beaters are collected and the tiger, which is pretty sure to remain in the neighbourhood of the kill, is driven out, the sportsmen being posted on small bamboo ladders from eight to ten feet high, placed against the stems of trees, as the tiger scarcely ever looks up, and though you may be sitting with your feet unpleasantly near the ground it does not appear to notice you. I certainly never heard an instance of any one being *pulled* off a ladder by a tiger, but a curious accident happened to an officer I was acquainted with. He fired at a tiger that was coming straight up to him; on receiving the shot it bounded forward, struck the ladder and brought the unfortunate shooter down on to its back, very much as a cocoanut at a fair is brought down from the top of a stick; the brute then seized him by the thigh and carried him off, eventually dropping him, frightened by the shouting of the men. My friend was fortunately only bitten through the fleshy part of the thigh and soon recovered, but never again, I believe, got back his nerve.

A young Scotchman, who was a first rate shot, having had a good deal of experience in Highland deer shooting before he came out to India, joined a regiment in this neighbourhood, and accompanied some of his brother officers on a tiger shooting trip. You may be pretty sure he was not posted in the most likely run; however, there are few things more uncertain in this life than the direction wild animals will take when driven. My young friend had only been a short time on his ladder when a tiger came; a steady well-placed shot dropped him dead. He had only just reloaded when up came a bear, and he hit him very hard; the bear seeing the body of the tiger in front of him immediately attacked it, and while so occupied was easily finished off. Then before the end of the beat another tiger came past his tree, giving him a broadside shot as it went by he felt pretty sure he had hit that also—no other shots were fired. When the beat was over, the old hands came up to him with, "Well, youngster, what have you been doing? we heard a lot of shots." The youngster quietly replied, "Oh, I have been rather lucky; there is a tiger and a bear down there, and I think you will find another tiger beyond;" and sure enough there was the other tiger lying dead. One can imagine their surprise, not to mention other feelings, at the Griffin's bag on his first day's tiger shooting! Alas! Dame Fortune did not smile upon us as she did on him; we went to the most likely places we could hear of, and posted bullocks night after night, but we only succeeded in getting one "kill." Bad luck still clung to us, for after posting us, as the men were leaving, they disturbed the tiger, who with an angry roar dashed into the jungle in front of us, and as he stood at about sixty yards from my tree, I had a splendid sight of the magnificent brute, but I would not fire, because he was right in the line of the beaters, and I was in hopes they would drive him nearer. However, after standing for about half a minute he moved into the thick jungle; soon afterwards the beaters commenced shouting, and I saw him stealing away to my left about a hundred yards distant, in a direction quite away from the beat, and from the trees where we were posted. I could not resist giving him a shot, though there was an uncertainty at that distance of bagging him, and a danger to the beaters if he was only wounded. I fancied I had hit, for he gave two roars as if in pain and dashed on; I afterwards saw the marks where he had struck his claws into the ground when I fired, but we soon lost his track. We had another beat on the chance of finding him. The next day I sent some men to look him up; they followed the track for some distance and noticed that the tiger had gone away on three legs. From what I know now I should say the beast was hit, for I never knew or heard of a tiger leaving the marks of his claws on the ground

AN UNEXPECTED MEETING.

unless he was wounded, as he cannot afford to blunt them. This was the only tiger we saw, except one which my companion Watson came upon quite suddenly; he was looking over a bank into a nullah, when he saw a large tiger lying down quite close to him; the brute was wide awake, got up, walked up the bank and stood staring at him for some time, within fifteen yards. Watson very wisely refrained from firing, although his shikarie urged him to do so; at last to his great relief the tiger walked quietly away, and after going a few paces broke into a trot and disappeared amongst the bamboos.

We visited the forest again in June, on a short trip of ten days, but the monsoon set in and spoilt our sport, or more correctly the sport was not up to our anticipations. We had rather an exciting incident on our way home. The natives turn their ponies loose on the outskirts of the forest during the monsoon, for grazing; these "tats" as they are called, are half wild, and many of them the most vicious brutes you can imagine; we suddenly found ourselves in the midst of a drove of them, and the moment they saw us they came charging down on us with loud neighs; there was nothing for it but to bolt. Two ponies came after me, and it was as much as I could do to keep out of their clutches; a bite in the thigh from one of these brutes would be no joke. As I doubled and turned from them I could not help thinking of the poor hares and foxes I was so fond of coursing, and the two open-mouthed ponies on my flanks gave me some idea of what the hares and foxes must feel when chased by my dogs. Eventually by dodging round a bush I managed to baffle my pursuers and joined my two companions, who had also been chased, but not so perseveringly as I was. We had utterly lost the points of the compass, and in wandering about to find our road we came upon the ponies again, but fortunately saw them without their having seen us, and escaped in safety.

CHAPTER IV.

SINGAPORE—JAVA—LABUAN.

SINGAPORE—POORNESS OF SPORT—SHOOT THE ONLY STAG—CHINESE AND TIGERS—AFTER RHINOCEROS—NO SUCCESS—CURIOUS MISTAKE—THE ARGUS PHEASANT—PADDLING MY OWN CANOE—NATIVES SPEARING THE SEER FISH—OBTAIN THREE MONTHS' LEAVE TO VISIT JAVA—TAKEN FOR A SPY—KINDNESS OF THE GOVERNOR GENERAL—TOO MUCH CARE TAKEN OF ME—OFFICIALS' FEAR OF MY BEING KILLED BY TIGERS AND LITTLE SPORT IN CONSEQUENCE—GREAT QUANTITIES OF GAME OF ALL SORTS—TWO KINDS OF WILD HOG—EXCURSION TO THE EASTERN PART OF THE ISLAND—VISIT THE VOLCANOES, SMEROE AND BROMO—A CHANCE OF A TIGER—SECURE A PEACOCK'S TAIL—MISS A CHANCE AT A LEOPARD—THE BROMO, MARVELLOUS VIEW—THE CRATER AND THE SANDY SEA—THE TENGGER RANGE—THE HILL PONIES—ERUPTION OF THE KLUTI—TEMPLES OF BLEETA AND SOOKOO—CITY OF SOERAKATA—AUDIENCE WITH THE EMPEROR—TIGER FIGHT—TEMPLE OF BOROBODOO—ADVENTURE WITH A PYTHON—AFTER A RHINOCEROS BY MOONLIGHT—NATIVE MODE OF TAKING GAME—OUT AFTER DEER—MY LAST STAG AND THE QUAGMIRE—THE AXIS DEER—STORY OF A TIGER—LABUAN—AT FIRST SIGHT NOT CHEERFUL—THE PIRATE AND HIS SEVEN HUNDRED MEN—NARROW ESCAPE OF THE BARRACKS FROM FIRE—DENSITY OF THE FOREST—DIFFICULTY OF FINDING ONE'S WAY—ANECDOTE OF THE SEA CAPTAIN—THE BIG BOAR OF LABUAN—CURIOUS BEES' NESTS.

SINGAPORE with its valleys, plains, grand trees and undulating hills, is very beautiful. In 1846 a great portion of the settlement was covered with jungle so dense that it was almost impenetrable and sport was hopeless. There were some deer, muntjack or barking deer, and wild hog on the island, and we managed after many a blank day, to kill a few of these. I was fortunate in shooting the only stag of any size that had been killed on the island for a long time, and the advantage of not wearing any conspicuous color when out after game was very manifest on this occasion. We were posted by the side of the high road where the forest had been cleared and a scrub jungle had grown up. I saw the stag suddenly appear on some rising ground above the road and deliberately take his bearings. Now as all my companions had something white about them which made them very conspicuous, and I had nothing of the kind visible, he came straight down to where I was standing, and on his coming within shot got the contents of both my barrels which turned him back severely wounded, and he fell dead after proceeding a short distance; a fine beast, 13 hands at the shoulder with small but very thick antlers. They tell me that the deer on the island never have very large antlers. My sporting friends after this event, took great pains to hide every scrap of white in their dress, but no more stags came to be shot. There was said to be a great number of tigers on the island and some hundreds of Chinamen were reported to be killed each year by them, but as the Chinamen belonged to secret societies who were in perpetual feud and always ready to kill each other, I am afraid many a murder has been falsely attributed to the "gentleman in stripes." In respect to this, I was told rather an amusing story of a very knowing Chinaman. The stems of the large cable-like creepers that twine about the forest trees like huge snakes, are valuable on account of their variety of colour and beauty of grain, for wood veneering; the above mentioned individual having found a spot where these valuable creepers abounded and fearing that others might reap the harvest, adopted an ingenious plan to keep them away; he carefully carved a tiger's foot in wood and stamped the impression in every direction leading to this piece of jungle; after a time news was brought in by another wood cutter of these numerous tracks; on first visiting the ground there appeared to be little doubt as to its being much frequented by a tiger, but on carefully inspecting the foot prints, it was discovered that they were *all made by one foot.*

I offered large rewards to get a shot at a tiger, but though I often sat up for one I never once had a chance. There was however some very fair snipe shooting to be got in the cultivated grounds.

I made a short expedition to some high ground on to the main land beyond Jahore; it was all through forest, and we more than once came across fresh tracks of rhinoceros. I was most anxious to shoot one of these beasts and kept an eager look out, but though on our return we saw their fresh tracks obliterating our footmarks, fortune did not favour us. On this occasion shortly after passing these tracks, I thought I was going to have a bit of good luck; I was advancing some distance in front of the rest of the party, when I spied up a vista in the forest, what I thought was a rhinoceros standing by a tree; I could only see its head and ear, the tree hiding the rest of the body. I could see the ear distinctly moving backwards and forwards. Making signs to the people to stop, with beating heart I crept from tree to tree, and when I at last came within range, imagine my disappointment on finding that the ear was a solitary dead leaf and that the head was a combination of a dead branch and a bush; the leaf being moved by the wind gave it such a life like appearance that I was very nearly firing at it, and it thoroughly deceived me as well as the natives with me. The lights and shades in the forest, combined with dead branches, bushes, &c., take at times such curious shapes that the wonder is mistakes are not oftener made. I once mistook a bush for a pea fowl and actually did fire a charge of shot into it. From the numerous calls I heard around me there appeared to be a great many of that rare and beautiful bird the argus pheasant, and being most anxious to secure a specimen, I stalked to the sound most cautiously, but I never even got a glimpse of these wary birds. We were much tormented by the little forest leeches which, although not bigger than a rose caterpillar, appeared to cover the ground and hang on every leaf ready to fix themselves on us; at one place we had continually to move on, being afraid to make a halt on account of them; we were duly protected with leech gaiters but they got down the back of our necks and up our sleeves; how the natives, who had no protection, escaped being absolutely sucked dry is a puzzle to me.

One of my chief amusements at Singapore was "paddling my own canoe" amongst the lovely islands and looking down into the coral covered depths below, which on a calm day seemed like a fairy forest, the coral having a most tree-like appearance and of every variety of tint from deep red to the most delicate green. Fish of all sizes and colors were swimming about in every direction far down in these charming water woods. So clear is the sea that the Malays in their sanpans, a very light kind of canoe, chase and spear the seer fish, which here takes the place of salmon, only the flesh is white instead of pink. It is a fast swimmer, quite as large as the salmon and excellent eating. Two Malays, one in the bow and the other in the stern of the canoe, paddle out in search of the fish and on finding a shoal give chase; the man at the bow, besides his paddle, has a long three pronged bamboo spear, like an eel spear, and wears a large shade over his eyes to assist him in seeing into the depths below. The pace they go and the turns and doubles they make is very exciting, and the excitement increases when the man at the bow stands up and with the spear balancing above his head prepares to strike—now he is going to throw! No! he calmly puts the spear down and paddles with all his might at one time passing close to you, then dashing off far away, suddenly doubling back again—now he is up once more, and the spear quivers in his hand. Now! Now! No, he calmly lays down the spear again and is paddling away as hard as ever. This sometimes is repeated over and over again and my patience has been sorely tried when looking on, the calm unexcited bearing of the spearman making it still more provoking. At last the spear is thrown and with such unerring aim that I have never to my recollection seen a failure. The spear is heavily weighted at the base so that it throws up the fish, and being made fast to the boat by a line is easily hauled in. I have seen fish of between 20 and 30 lbs. captured in this way. It is also interesting to watch the ospreys or fishing eagles, of which there were numbers, soaring high above and dropping like a bullet into the sea, rising again with a good sized fish in their talons.

I became very tired of the life at Singapore; the monotonous climate, a kind of perpetual hot house summer, and the lack of sport, made me apply for three months' leave to Java, and great was my joy on obtaining it. It was on the 10th May, 1848 that I embarked on board the Dutch steamer for Batavia. Soon after my arrival I found that sport must be a secondary consideration if I wished to visit the most interesting portions of one of the most lovely islands in the world, as I could not afford the time to remain stationary. I happened to arrive in Java at a most exciting period; the great European revolutions had just burst into flame, and the Dutch had made up their minds that the English Government if driven to war with France would take it from them; my arrival, therefore, created quite a sensation; there was a very strong suspicion amongst the good people of Batavia that I was an English spy, and they could not understand why the Governor General was so civil to me, granting me permission to travel all over the island; moreover issuing an order that Captain Hamilton was to be treated with every attention.

I met with great kindness at Government House. Colonel Butterworth, the Governor of Singapore, by having the Java mails made up separately saved the Batavian Government the trouble and expense of sending all the way to Hong Kong for their letters, for which act of consideration the Governor General was very grateful, and my arrival in the island shortly afterwards with a letter of introduction from the Colonel, enabled his Excellency to show through me his appreciation of the kind act of our Governor; hence the mystery of my reception which so puzzled the public at large. At various places I reviewed troops, made speeches, and was driven about escorted by cavalry, and I gratefully acknowledge the kindness and civility I received from all the Government Officials during my sojourn in the Island. Unfortunately in the circular order issued, it was mentioned that I was to be shown sport; in some places whole districts were turned out to beat the jungles for me, but as a rule the

Dutch civilian of those days was not a sportsman and had no idea of the necessity of keeping perfectly quiet when a beat was taking place; the consequence was that though game abounded, I got but very few shots. They generally posted me with a couple of belted officials to look after me, who when they heard anything approaching would insist upon calling to me to look out, thereby turning the animal back. I used to steal away from them and by dodging about in the jungle, hoped to shake them off, but no, perhaps just as some animal was approaching, these noisy officials would come upon me! My fury would be great, but it had not the slightest effect upon them. They were ordered to keep me in sight and did so. So fearful were they that I should be killed by a tiger or a rhinoceros that they would not let me go anywhere alone; not that they cared so much about me individually, but if anything happened they would have to report it to the Governor General; indeed one official on hearing that I had gone out alone with my rifle said to the English planter with whom I was staying, "Oh dear, oh dear! he will be killed by a tiger and I shall have to report it to the Governor General!" and his delight on seeing me walk in with a whole skin was really sincere and genuine. Many parts of the island swarmed with wild hog, and some of the old boars were very savage. They were of a species of wart hog,[1] though differing considerably from the African species, and when facing you their body is completely hidden by their huge ugly heads. I killed a good many of them, besides muntjack, pea fowl, jungle fowl and a few deer[2] of the larger kind but smaller than our Indian sambur.

[1] There are two species of wild hog in Java, *Sus verrucosus* or wart hog and *Sus vittatus*.

[2] *Cervus rusa*.

I often got shots at all the above from the high road by stopping the carriage and jumping out.

After remaining a short time in Batavia and its neighbourhood, and being very anxious to see as much as I could, the Governor General offered me a passage to Soerabaya on

WART HOG OF JAVA (Sus verrucosus).

the eastern coast of the island, near which town a friend of mine had a sugar mill. With him I remained some time making most interesting excursions to the Tengger mountains and to the volcanoes of the Bromo and the Smeroe. I was fortunate to be accompanied by a very pleasant travelling companion who knew the language and the district. The scenery was very fine, the mountains, nearly all of them volcanic, rise directly from the sea level and have a very grand and imposing effect. At one place, the muddy path along which we travelled, with high grass on each side and occasional patches of forest, was so beaten down with tiger tracks that it looked as if some one had been driving them like a flock of sheep to the market, and as I was most anxious to bag a Javanese tiger, we had a machan (platform) built commanding the most frequented of these tracks, and I sat up all one beautiful moonshiny night, but nothing came of it, and the only tiger I saw in these parts was lying out on rather a bare spot surrounded with high grass and well situated for a stalk; my guide made signs as if asking me whether I would shoot it; I replied "why certainly" as plain as I could by signs, so he beckoned me to dismount and follow him; we crept away through the grass, I all the time fancying he was bringing me round for a shot, at last I saw that he was taking me right away in a contrary direction. I then seized him by the scruff of his neck and made signs that we must go back and shoot the tiger; but the tiger settled the question by quietly walking into the jungle close at hand.

When I returned to the bungalow I had the man questioned as to whether he intended to take me up to the tiger. "What!" said he, "do you suppose I was going to let the gentleman shoot at the tiger? Why, if the tiger had killed him, what would have become of me?" One evening I made a very good stalk and shot a doe muntjack; I sent my guide with it to where the ponies were posted, and while waiting for his return I saw a peacock in grand plumage fly across and settle on the bare branch of a high tree that rose out of the centre of a very tigerish looking ravine. It was a long shot, but I could not resist having a crack at it with the rifle, when to my surprise down it went to the bottom of the ravine like a falling comet. I hesitated at first to enter such a place, but after a minute or two decided on going down. The jungle became thicker and thicker, I was at last obliged to crawl on my hands and knees; I had got down some distance when I distinctly heard some animal stealthily moving ahead of me. Reader, have you ever felt the "creepy creepy?" It comes up the calves of the legs, into the back, plays round the throat with a choky gulpy sensation and finishes off on the top of the head. I felt it in full force when I heard that movement, and I paused and listened most intently. To retreat was more dangerous than to push on, so on I went. The jungle was rather more open when I got under the big tree, but for the life of me I could not find the peacock. Darkness was setting in and I was in despair, and just as I was on the point of giving it up, I spied the bird lying dead. I lost no time in docking him of his splendid tail and scrambled up out of the ugly ravine as quickly as I could, and a comfortable feeling of relief came over me when I found myself on safe ground again.

I went out several mornings to look for deer, but the grass was so high that though mounted on ponies we could scarcely see above it. I got one or two unsatisfactory shots, having to scramble off the pony and fire, the high grass and other things being against a correct aim; how we like to make excuses when we fail to bag, as was often the case on these occasions. My greatest regret was losing a lovely chance at a leopard, when after a herd of deer. I could just see their heads above the long grass, and as they passed on the other side of a tree with low projecting branches that stood rather in the open, I tried to steal up under cover of it. When about 40 or 50 yards from the tree, I saw something move in the branches. It appeared to be a black monkey of which there were a great many in the jungle, so I took no more notice of it. I had not advanced more than ten paces, when down it dropped from the tree, and as it passed through the sunlight I saw the spots of a leopard. My disgust was intense. I ran up as hard as I could but the brute had sneaked away through the long grass, and my running forward frightened the deer, so I lost both.

As it was considered *infra dig.* for an officer in my position to travel in any other way than in a carriage, so long as I remained on the high roads I was obliged to submit, but as we approached the mountains, or whenever from various reasons we had to leave the main road, we had to take to our horses, a much more pleasant mode of proceeding. As we approached the Tengger range of hills with the mighty Smeroe, the highest volcano in Java, rising abruptly 12,000 feet in a huge cone, the scenery became very grand, and the mountain had a very imposing effect; this precipitous cone at that time had never been ascended, although several attempts had been made. During the time we were waiting for horses I amused myself in making a rough sketch of the magnificent view at the back of the bungalow at Paparawang, which was situated about 50 feet above the river, which at this time of the year (July) was like a trout stream at home, twisting and turning about in all directions, through a beautiful green valley; beyond which are coffee plantations and rice fields, and

THE SMEROE, FROM PAPARAWANG.

beyond those, in the middle distance, the jungle, or rather forest, which climbs up almost to the summit of the Tengger mountains, whose steep sides shut out all beyond, as a wall. At one end, as it were, of this, rises this great volcano with its summit puffing out a light cotton-like vapour, and half way down its precipices fleecy clouds were floating. The whole scene was most enchanting, far beyond my powers of description.

Immediately after leaving the village we began to ascend; for the first mile or two the view of the country below us was very beautiful, we could see Pooza and the island in front of it very distinctly. We then entered the thick forest; in many places we passed through gigantic ferns with the stems of the trees covered with a beautiful fine moss, the path and all the ground around carpeted with various coloured flowers. After a considerable ascent during which we were obliged to get off our ponies and walk through some stunted jungle amongst which strawberries and raspberries were growing in the greatest profusion, we came out on to open downs covered with ferns and long grass with here and there a pretty clump of trees. The buffaloes and horses grazing about indicated that we were approaching the village where we intended to bivouack for the night. The cold bracing air, the sight of the dog rose, blackberry and thistle growing on each side of the road, together with the fern-clad hills, made the eleven thousand miles vanish as it were as by the touch of a magician's hand, and I fancied I was again in my own dear native land. A little further on a turn of the road brought us suddenly in sight of a pretty little mountain village snugly sheltered in a dell below us, backed by gardens and picturesque clumps of trees. On nearer approach we found the beauty of the village was best seen at a distance, it being nothing but a miserable cluster of huts with one larger than the rest constituting our hotel. Immediately on arriving the people brought cups of hot water for us to drink, but my companion explained to them that we did not care for that kind of beverage, so they then brought a dish of smoking hot potatoes, which was much more acceptable. The air was so cold that we found it difficult to keep ourselves warm till dinner time, and when that hour did arrive we were agreeably surprised to find an excellent hot repast placed before us. Our keen appetites would have relished a much worse fare, but everything was very well cooked and the dishes were piping hot. After satisfying ourselves I attempted to sketch some of the natives who crowded round us, but as soon as I got out my pencil they all ran away. These Tengger people, as they are called from the mountains they inhabit, are all Hindoos, the only tribe in Java that has not been converted to Mohammedanism. They are a fine robust race, very quiet and unoffending, and strange to say they are not a bit better clothed than the people of the plains, although they appear to suffer much from the cold; the sight of some of the children stark naked made me shiver; before we went to bed we were glad to warm ourselves at a fire the natives had lighted before the door. I had luckily brought with me a country made blanket, but with that even, I could get but little sleep, and was glad enough when morning dawned.

Soon after sunrise we started for the Bromo. I remained behind for a short time to make a hasty sketch of the hill village; but as I heard Symond's horn high above me, I hastened on, and at the spot where I overtook him the view was superb. He was standing on the spur of the mountain under some venerable cassuarina trees; on each side were deep ravines beautifully wooded, but the grand view of all was in the direction from which we had come. Away down, some thousand feet, was the village we had left with its variegated cod-roy looking gardens; beyond, the forest clad hills and dark ravines extended down, down, till the eye reached the plain below, and beyond again, the whole of the eastern part of the island was spread out like a map; we could see both the north and south coasts and could almost look into the crater of the Lamongan. It was, indeed, a glorious sight! Soon after, we approached the bare summit of the highest point we had to ascend; even the cassuarina trees did not grow here, nothing but a short kind of grass; just before arriving at the summit I left the path and rode up to the top of a rounded hill to see what there was beyond. A most extraordinary sight met my view; I looked down on the Bromo and the sandy sea a thousand feet below me. When I first beheld it, the so-called sea was covered with a beautiful gauze of clouds which gradually cleared away disclosing the broad expanse of sand. The steep wall of rock by which it is surrounded is covered with cassuarina trees, the beautiful green mountains in the centre, contrasting strongly with the one scorched and bare corner which forms the present crater of the Bromo, and presenting the most beautiful and at the same time most extraordinary scene I had ever beheld. I stood upon nearly the highest part of the outer wall, as it may be called, and in front of me was a desert of sand, many miles in extent.

At the furthest right hand corner of the mass of mountains is the volcano of the Bromo, bleak and scorched,

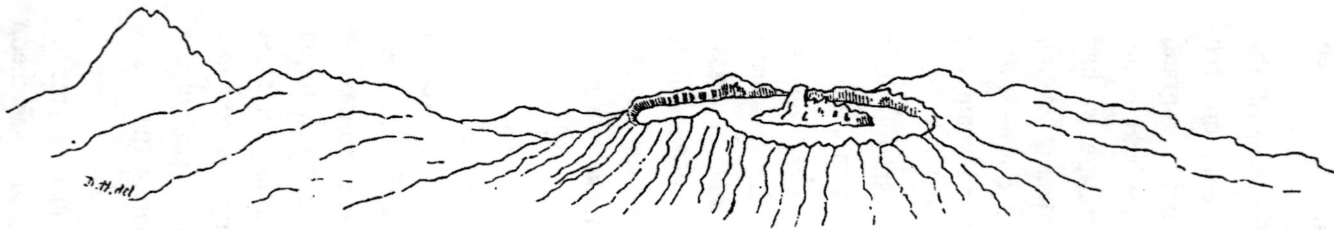

BIRDSEYE VIEW OF THE CRATER OF THE BROMO.
Shewing the Sandy Sea and the precipitous circular wall which surrounds it.

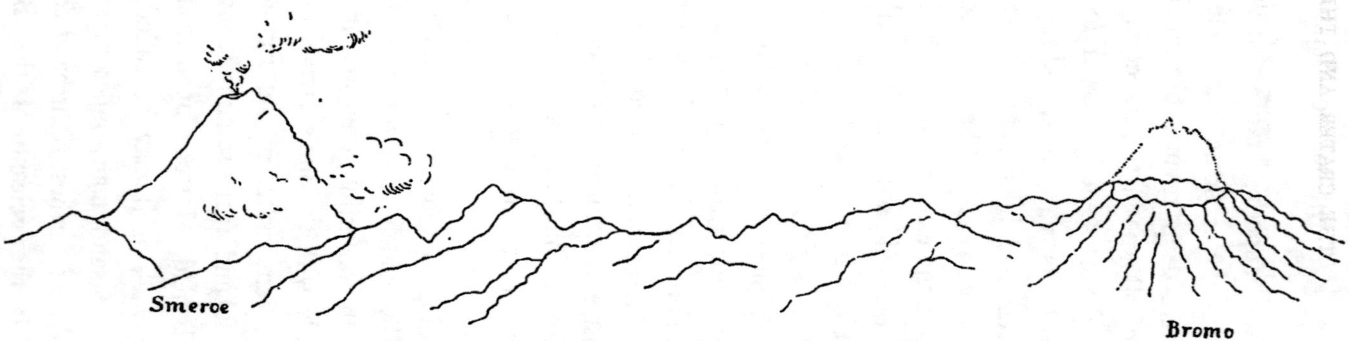

OUTLINE OF THE SMEROE AND THE BROMO.
The dotted line on the Bromo shewing the supposed original shape of the mountain.

looking the very picture of desolation. I could almost imagine it was a portion of the mountain that from some cause had become withered and died away; all the hills around it were so beautiful and green, while this was a bare heap of ashes and sand without a blade of grass upon it, and on one side, where the mud and sand had been thrown out the rains had furrowed them into hundreds of miniature mountains and ravines. It is supposed that originally the mountain rose up in the shape of a cone similar to that of the Smeroe, and that in the course of time it undermined itself and in some great eruption burst and fell in; the remains of the upper portion of the mountain became embedded in the centre of the sand which must have been collected in the crater of the old volcano, at the same time the outer surface of the old volcano became a circular range of nearly perpendicular hills completely surrounding the sandy plain. To give some idea of this volcano and its curious formation, imagine a tea cup or circular bowl with the rim broken and jagged; fill it two-thirds full of fine sand, and place a piece of pumice stone in the centre, bank up the outer surface of the cup to about one third of the top, the rim will represent the jagged wall, the sand the sandy sea, as it is called, and the pumice stone the present crater, which is about 7,359 feet above the sea level. I remained a short time to make a sketch, and we then rode along the jagged ridge of the outer wall for about four or five miles; in many places the path was not more than five feet broad, with a precipice of a thousand feet on one side, and from four to five hundred feet on the other. The scenery was magnificent beyond description. We had a fine view of the Smeroe all the time; it did not look above five or six miles distant, but was in reality I believe, about twenty; when we were at the nearest point to it, it threw out a splendid puff of smoke or ashes, as white as snow, in the shape of a tree, or more like a huge cauliflower of superfine wool. At first I felt very uncomfortable riding along the narrow path, more especially at one spot where we turned suddenly at nearly a right angle. I felt exactly as if the saddle was going to slip over the pony's head; besides, the pony would crop the grass just on the very edge of the precipice, but I was told to give him his head, as these ponies were so sure-footed that there was no danger. My companion's pony actually had the audacity to shy, at a place where there was barely sufficient room to turn round. By degrees I got used to it, and could look at the tops of the trees a thousand feet below me without a shudder. We descended to the sandy sea at a place where the wall was not quite so perpendicular, and proceeded to the crater. The sand is quite hard, as fine as drifted snow, and in many places the wind had formed it into waves and ridges exactly similar to a snow drift. On one side, the plain is covered with hundreds of stones, some very large, which have been thrown out from the volcano. I rode through the desolate looking ravines formed amongst the lava to within a couple of hundred feet of the edge of the crater, and when I got to the top the sight I saw made me almost tumble backwards. I looked right into a hole, a *bowl* would be more expressive, nearly a mile across, between three and four miles in circumference, and said to be fifteen hundred feet deep; I could see right to the bottom of the crater, which was not even smoking; the awful stillness of this fearful pit was quite appalling, yet I could not tear myself away from the spot, it was so terribly grand. In returning I had again to cross the sandy sea, and ascended the outer wall at its lowest point where its height is not above three or four hundred feet; the wind had risen, and the fine sand cut my face considerably. I noticed the tracks of a wild boar, it must have been a very solitary boar indeed to have chosen such a country to travel over.

I was much struck with the hill ponies we had on this trip. They are very small, about the size of, perhaps a trifle larger, than Shetland ponies, but very powerful and enduring. Some of these ponies from the neighbouring islands are splendid thoroughbred looking animals; four of them belonging to my host of the Mill (Mr. Etty) were bright bays, and as handsome as they could be: we drove them in a light carriage and they went like the wind.

We descended the other side of the mountain to a bungalow situated on a delightful spot in an opening between the mountains on the road to Probolingoo. A pensioned Dutch soldier was in charge. We were capitally housed and fed, and I remember a dish of peaches being particularly good. The next morning we descended to the foot of the mountains where we found the above named ponies and carriage, and were at Monolangan Mill by noon.

Before leaving the eastern part of the island I made an excursion to the Lake of Ranio Clakka, a lovely piece of water supposed to have been the crater of an extinct volcano, surrounded on all sides by a dense forest, from which rises to the height of about 4,000 feet, the almost inaccessible precipices and pyramidal summit of the Lamongan. This volcano, although always emitting smoke, seldom breaks out into eruption; when however this does occur, it is always preceded by the summit becoming extremely pointed. When I made my visit this was the case, but although the mountain was very uneasy and every now and again sent forth volumes of smoke, with violent explosions as if hundreds of cannon were being fired simultaneously,. causing us to rush out of the bungalow in the greatest hurry, our hopes were always disappointed.

I waited as long as I possibly could, and of course, some short time after I left, on one calm night the critical period arrived, and about three hundred feet of the summit was blown off, and numerous streams of molten lava coursed down the precipitous sides of the mountain. It was one of the finest eruptions that had been seen, and those who witnessed it, described the scene, reflected in the mirror-like surface of the lake, as splendid in the extreme. Fortunately the eruptions of this mountain do little or no harm, as the flow of the lava does not extend much beyond the cone.

Towards the end of July I bade adieu to my kind and hospitable friends, and started overland for Batavia. The first part of the journey I was accompanied by a very agreeable Englishman who had settled in Java, but the latter part I had to make alone in my carriage. I used to travel with my rifle by my side, and managed to bag a good many wild hog as well as peafowl and jungle fowl, which were as common as possible all along the route, and afforded excellent sport.

A few days before I arrived at Kediri there had been an eruption of the Kluti (Kloet), a volcano 5,193 feet above the sea, and when I came to the bank of the river I was nearly pitched into it in consequence of the coachman attempting to drive over a temporary structure made of bamboo framework, to replace a part of the bridge which had been carried away by the flood. The effects of the late

LAKE OF RANIO CLAKKA.

eruption were evident in all directions. Mr. La Rona told me that there must have been upwards of half a mile of drift timber collected against the bridge, which forcing its way through, destroyed the greater part of the structure, the massive brick portion having been pushed bodily out of its position. They told me that the water of the river at Kediri, although some thirty miles distant from the volcano, was so hot on the night of the eruption that the hand placed in it could scarcely be kept there a moment. An immense mass of boiling mud and water was carried down, intermixed with thousands of dead and dying fish, parboiled bodies of tigers, banting, deer, monkeys and wild pigs, the torrent of boiling water having flowed over some eight miles of jungle before it arrived at the tributary stream and thence into the Kediri river. Several villages were destroyed, but happily few lives, as the villagers had warning, and had taken flight at the first rumblings of the mountain. By all accounts the eruption must have been a most awful sight, the loud concussions and reports were like a tremendous cannonade with intervals of small arms firing, like a naval engagement, so much so that in many places the natives had the idea that the English had arrived and were taking the island. The sound appeared to travel only in one direction, along the line of mountains to the west; at Soerabaja to the east, the first intimation of anything going on was the mass of mud, carcases of dead animals and drift timber brought down by the river—not a sound had been heard.

At Kediri I called on the Regent, who has a very nice house; he is reported to be a dashing fellow, and will sit up and drink and play at cards with you as long as you like. He holds the rank of captain in one of the Dutch regiments, and professes to be a great sportsman. He showed me his guns, and amongst them a very nice rifle; he also made his people bring the legs of a banting which had been killed the day before by one of his men with a spear; the man went into the jungle to cut wood when he saw something move just ahead of him, he threw his spear at it, and much to his astonishment, found he had killed a full grown cow banting, the spear having, fortunately for him, severed the spinal marrow.

I was anxious to visit a curious temple lately discovered near the foot of the Kluti, and started soon after sunrise with Mr. La Rona for Bleeta. On the road we saw the immense amount of devastation caused by the ashes which fell during the eruption.

The Bleeta temple, the original shape of which I cannot determine, is now a square mass of ruin with three terraces or platforms, the walls of which are most superbly carved in high relief, portraying different ceremonies and processions. Each tablet is separated from the next by a circular ornament, in the centre of which is some animal exquisitely carved. I noticed nearly every animal common to Java, as well as carvings of the elephant, the camel and the cassowary; in all the figures the proportions were very correct. It was remarkable how very curiously the roots of the trees have eaten up as it were some of the smaller temples or gateways, and what was still more curious, the trees and roots had in some instances put on the form of the temples they had destroyed. Some rascally Mohamedan fanatics have mutilated every human figure in the temples by cutting off the noses. I believe this is universal. In all the temples in Java there is hardly a single figure with a perfect nose. The monsters! I should like to have the grinding of their noses.

At Madioen, where I arrived on July 23rd, I was invited by the Regent to be present at a kind of field day held by him once a month. He is a prince of the royal blood, and the highest native in the Dutch service. All his attendants were in their court dresses, that is, naked to the waist. Some sixty horsemen rather handsomely dressed with curious caps passed round in review, after which they enacted a kind of tournament, each couple performing a lance exercise as they passed the Regent at full gallop. It had a very pretty effect.

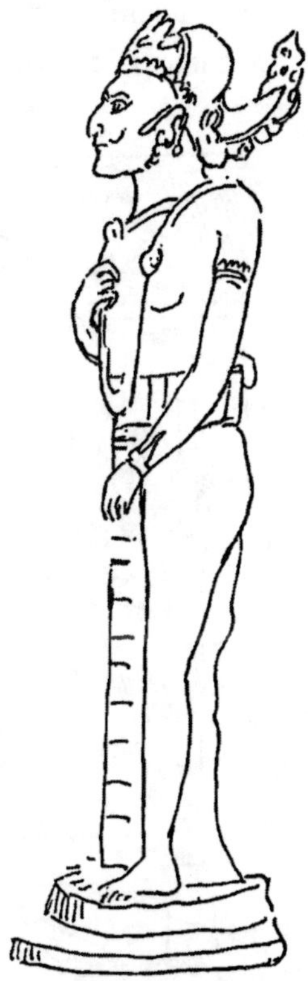

Principal figure in the Temple of Sookoo.

On the road from Madioen, I visited the famous temple of Sookoo or Sokowati; we had to leave the main road, so mounted our horses and had a most beautiful ride over the mountain side to within a quarter of a mile of the Temple, which is quite different to anything I have yet seen, and for a wonder several of the figures have their faces perfect. Three stone slabs showing the making of the kriss were very curious, and the principal figure in the temple was quite perfect. After finishing my sketches, I went down to the entrance gate and stood at the edge of the hill beyond. I could have stood there for hours looking at the magnificent scene before me. It was worth coming any distance, if only to stand on that spot on a bright sunshiny afternoon.

The next day I arrived at Solo, the popular name of the

city of Soerakata, about four p.m., and put up at the hotel, had my dinner, and took a stroll in the evening. The town is pleasantly situated, with a river, the Solo, running through it. There is a very fine and broad avenue of tamarind trees leading up to the emperor's palace, and some of the banyan

D.H., Java, July, 1848.

THREE STONE SLABS AT THE TEMPLE OF SOOKOO, SHEWING THE MANUFACTURE OF THE KRISS.

trees in other parts of the town are magnificent specimens. These trees are generally planted in the centre of the Allon-Allon, the Javanese name for the open square before all the houses of the great men, on which they have their tiger fights, and parades of troops, &c. The city, placed in a flat plain, is surrounded by distant mountains which tower to the sky and have a very fine effect. The next day I had to put on my full dress to visit the Emperor, accompanied by a Colonel of the Dutch Artillery and his wife. The two wives of the Emperor were also present, with his daughter and daughter-in-law; none of these ladies were beauties, but they were covered with fine jewels. The Emperor was rather neatly dressed à la Javanese, with some Dutch order on his breast. He was a man about middle age and not very bright looking. There was quite a swarm of half naked children squatting behind the chairs of the ladies. His Imperial Majesty is always waited upon by women who shortly after our arrival brought in tea; his handmaidens were not beautiful, so that I did not regret having my tea handed to me by two half castes of the male sex dressed up in a kind of rifle uniform with tails to their coats. The Emperor's band was playing all the time of our audience; the band is composed entirely of Javanese and played remarkably well. Shortly after tea we took our departure. I am unfortunate in being here at the commencement of the Ramadan, as otherwise I should most likely have been present at a tiger fight which, from what they tell me, is worth seeing. They have two modes of attacking the tiger, one is with the buffalo and the other by spearing. The first is similar to the Indian buffalo fights; but the latter is peculiar to Java. The tiger is set down in a trap in the centre of the Allon-Allon, surrounded by a triple or quadruple line of spearmen about a hundred yards distant from the trap. When all is ready a Javanese armed with a kriss advances at a very slow pace, to the sound of soft music, and sets fire to the trap, at the same time opening the door which is at the back part of the cage which is too narrow for the tiger to turn in. As the fire begins to singe his whiskers he gradually backs out. The man as soon as he has opened the door, commences returning towards the crowd, at the same slow pace and the slower he returns the more applause he gains. The tiger having backed out of his burning prison is rather astonished at finding himself surrounded by hundreds of people each pointing a spear at him. If he is a bold tiger he canters round the circle almost touching the spears; finding no opening he returns to the centre, fixes his eye on one spot and with a loud roar dashes straight at it. He is received on the spears, and though he crushes many as if they were mere reeds, in half a minute he falls dead, pierced with a hundred wounds. In some instances however, the roar and the charge is too much for the Javanese and they give way. The sport then becomes rather dangerous to the lookers on.[1]

On the second of August, I drove to Djokjakarta, forty-nine miles from Solo, visiting the Temples of Prambanan on the way. The first I came to was one of the Thousand Temples, a mass of large ruins surrounded by an infinite number of smaller ones. The four entrance gates are each guarded by two large figures, beautifully carved out of one solid piece of stone; further on, I came upon two very fine

[1] Le Comte De Beauvoir "Voyage Autour du Monde," gives a description of the tigers which are kept for these fights. After having been caught they are shut up for fifteen days and fed on the carcases of dogs, sheep, and offal of all kinds. The stench from this is perfectly unbearable. They seem to lose, by this treatment, nearly all their courage, and few of them show any severe fighting.

Mr. Beete Jukes, the naturalist to the surveying vessel "Fly," Captain Blackwood, witnessed one of these tiger fights with a buffalo. The tiger appeared very mangy and half starved and was soon put *hors de combat.*

figures of Buddhist Priests beautifully carved; not being up in Buddhist lore, I cannot say who they were, but one was the gentleman with the elephant's head so common in India. On the 3rd I went to see the graves of the Sultans, and in the evening had an audience with the reigning Sultan accompanied by the Resident. Being the Fast the palace was closed, but His Majesty received us in one of his pandopos with just enough light to make darkness visible. He is a young man, exceedingly fat. He had on a blue silk jacket which, with his fat stomach, gave him something of the appearance of a head waiter with a fancy jacket and apron. He has only one wife, reported to be a great beauty. I had the honour of an interview with her after the audience with her husband; she is certainly pretty, but nothing remarkable, quite young, with a very fair complexion, and fine black eyes, her skin looking as soft as velvet.

On the 4th of August I started for Magelang, and on the way visited the wonderful temple of Borobodoo. We first came to the temple of Mundort, discovered by Mr. Hartman in 1836 in rather a curious manner. It was buried several feet deep in ashes and mud deposited by different eruptions of the Merapi and Merbaboe volcanoes, and appeared like a small mound covered with trees and jungle. One of the trees on the summit attracted Mr. Hartman's eye from the beautiful flower it bore, and he ordered it to be taken up and transplanted to his garden. On getting at the roots some stones were dug up and the mound was reported hollow; there was a small opening left after the tree was taken up, but no one would go in for fear of cheetas or tigers. At last Mr. Hartman made one of his men creep in and see what was there. The man went in, and not coming out again he sent another in, who, catching hold of the first man's leg hauled him out. He was quite insensible, and when he recovered he declared that the devil lived inside for he had seen him. Torches were brought, the hole was enlarged and in went Mr. Hartman, when to his delight, he discovered a splendid statue of a Buddhist Priest praying in a sitting posture, thirteen feet in height, of exquisite workmanship and proportions, and quite perfect. Eventually he had the earth cleared away and this beautiful temple brought to light. The temples of Borobodoo, four miles further on, are of great size and filled with exquisite carvings and statues. The natives say these temples were never finished, but were destroyed by an earthquake. The Dutch Government is about to have drawings made of the chief figures and carvings which are in the great temple, which will require at least three years' hard work to accomplish. I had heard a great deal from Mr. Hartman of the Valley of the Kadu, but I never anticipated such a treat as the view from the temple gave me: mountain scenery of the wildest description varied with tracts of cultivated patches of every shade and colour, all blended together, making a scene so enthralling that it was late in the afternoon before I could tear myself away.

On one of these excursions I had rather an exciting adventure. I was looking in some high grass, for the track of a deer I had fired at, when I almost trod upon a huge python; the part of the body that I saw was as thick as my thigh, and it appeared to extend some length either way; I at once beat a retreat, but I had not gone far when I heard a rustle in the grass behind me; the creepy creepy feeling already described came over me, for I thought the snake had awoke, and like the giant in the fairy story of my boyhood with a "fee-fie-fo-fum," was coming after me; but the tips of a deer's antlers as it rushed through the high grass relieved my nerves. I do not know what one would do if a big python made up his mind to dine off you, but from the lightning quickness with which I have seen one seize a squirrel, one would not have much time to think about it.

When on this excursion, I had fired at and badly wounded a large boar, and thinking I could easily finish him with a spear, a sort of halbert, which the lopas who accompany the carriage are armed with, I took one and went in at the boar, who kept making half charges at me from a thick bush in which he had taken shelter. On receiving him on the point of the spear in one of these charges the wretched weapon crumpled up altogether. I dropped it and turned round for the gun, but the bearer had bolted, and there was nothing for it but to try to catch him. I heard the champing of the angry boar's tusks behind me, so I put on a spurt and soon overtook the runaway, and seizing the rifle stopped the boar.

I was much disappointed in not even seeing a single banting (wild bull). I have been close to them and their fresh footprints have often raised my hopes, only to be frustrated by some blundering attendants frightening them or by some other contretemps quite as annoying. I was also most anxious to shoot a rhinoceros; but again I was out of luck. One of these beasts had committed much havoc amongst the gardens of the neighbourhood where I was staying and one moonlight night we drove out to try and intercept him in a garden he frequented. It was a full moon, and we were full of hope. The watchers came to say the beast was in the garden, so out we sallied; it was as clear as day when we started, but we had to walk some distance and before we got to our destination a dark cloud came up and all was as black as Erebus; on entering the garden we heard something moving ahead of us, but it was so dark we could see nothing. We waited for it to clear, but as there was no sign of it doing so, we got into the carriage and drove away. We had not gone far when the moon burst forth again in all her glory, and we afterwards heard that the rhinoceros was seen standing in the road in full moonlight. My last hope now was on the Preanger Mountains, and in the swampy plain of Bandoeng. My leave was rapidly coming to an end so I hastened on my way.

The plain of Bandoeng is an elevated plateau some thirty miles in length, and varying between six and ten miles in breadth. It consists of a swampy black soil, the finest in Java they say, and covered with high reeds, called glagga, which are from thirteen to fifteen feet high, with here and there open plains of low allony-allony (a broad-bladed grass) up to a man's waist, with pools of stagnant water, some of these covering dangerous bogs. The plain abounds with deer, rhinoceros, tigers and hog. A hunting party a month ago, in one of their grand beats killed one hundred and twenty deer and a rhinoceros, but the poor brutes were hemmed in on every side and slaughtered like sheep, in a fold. On these occasions they collect a great number of beaters and surround a portion of the plain, gradually decreasing the circle; the sportsmen are mounted on the bare backs of ponies, as no saddles would stand the rush and scramble through these tough high reeds. The only weapon they use is a short heavy kind of sword, with

AFTER DEER, BANDOENG.

which they cut down both the deer and the rhinoceros, the latter occasionally showing fight and doing considerable damage to horses and riders.

On my first day we entered the deer ground soon after daylight, and after a short time came on a large open plain some miles in extent, covered with grass, interspersed with forests of reeds and trees; on this plain several herds of deer were feeding, a beautiful sight, the stags keeping far out of shot, and on catching sight of us, trotted out to reconnoitre. Every now and then one would stop, shake his antlered head, and dash back to the herd as if to warn them of approaching danger, when the whole clustering together and showing quite a forest of heads and horns, would dash into the reeds, and disappear long before we could get within shot. It was only by skirting the little bays and inlets of grass at the side of the reeds that we had any chance, and even then it was difficult to approach within two hundred yards. I shot badly, firing at too great distances and at snap running shots; in fact the rush of deer in all directions kept me in such a perpetual state of excitement that I could not be cool. As soon as the sun had got well up the deer entered the high reeds, and we could hear them bellowing like a lot of bulls. I never heard anything like it. In the course of the day some five or six deer were wounded, but owing to the denseness of the reeds it was impossible to follow them for any distance. While endeavouring to track a stag I had hit I heard some big animal rush away and struggling forward as rapidly as I could, I came upon the still warm couch of a rhinoceros; perhaps it was as well I had not encountered him in such a place. We came home pretty well knocked up, and I was glad enough, the next day being Sunday, to take a rest. On the Monday, with one of my Dutch friends, we started at four a.m. for the same ground, and were more fortunate. I bowled over a good stag at a hundred and fifty yards, and dropped another on his tracks at a hundred and eighty yards, my companion also killing a fine young stag. Just before giving up for the day I saw a stag moving away in the high grass; he stood for a moment and I took a steady aim; on the ball striking him he sprung up in the air and fell over on his back, but when I got to the place to my astonishment he was gone; we followed on his tracks, and we could see by the footmarks that he had dashed into a deep quagmire where, from the bubbles which were rising, it was evident that he had been completely swallowed up.

So ended my sport in Java, often carried on under great difficulties, principally from the fear constantly present amongst the natives and those conducting the beats that I might come to some kind of grief either by being bagged by a tiger or from some other cause, for which they would be made responsible.

Game exists in abundance, particularly deer and hogs. The deer are smaller than the Indian sambur, more like our Red deer in colour, but with the same number of tines on the antlers as the sambur. The stags have a habit of collecting masses of reeds and swamp grass on their antlers which gives them a fierce look as well as a very remarkable appearance when a number of them are moving together. There is only one locality in the neighbourhood of Cheribon, where the Axis or spotted deer is found in a wild state, but they are often kept in enclosures in the same manner as our fallow deer. If the grass had been burnt

I should probably have had much better sport, for when this is done the native sportsmen kill vast quantities of all kinds of game. Their mode of proceeding is as follows: They surround with ropes a large portion of ground including several clumps of forest trees and jungle. The deer and banting take shelter in these and are beaten out. The deer will not face the rope and numbers are cut down by

the horsemen. They never attempt to attack a bull banting, but the cows are sometimes killed in the melée.

The Banting (*Bos. sondaicus*), somewhat like our Indian bison only not so large and with smaller horns, is plentiful; the bulls are particularly fierce and dangerous. I had not a chance of coming across one, but have heard them close by me. The Muntjac Deer (*Cervulus muntjac*) is also plentiful; the native name for it is Kedang, and I managed to kill some of them amongst the high grass, but it was most difficult to take a correct aim.

Tigers and leopards are very numerous, but owing to the circumstances mentioned above I never saw but one tiger in a wild state. Those kept in confinement were fine large fellows but lean and ragged in appearance. A very extraordinary story of a tiger was told me which I believe to be perfectly true; it took place a few months since and is well authenticated. At a village where we stopped it is the custom to put the buffaloes under the charge of the native boys who take them out to their grazing ground in the morning and bring them back again in the evening. The boys generally choose one of the herd to ride upon, and the boy and the buffalo get much attached to each other. One morning a boy, whilst leading the herd was seized and carried off by a tiger. The pet buffalo and another immediately gave chase and made the tiger drop the boy, and as soon as he did so the pet buffalo ran up and stood over the boy remaining in this position till the other buffalo had driven the tiger well into the jungle. The poor boy was severely bitten in the shoulder but eventually recovered. The tiger was pursued and killed by the natives. Although they rather object to injure a tiger that has done no harm, the moment one attacks a human being or one of their cattle, they turn out *en masse*, shew most determined and persevering courage and rarely return without their victim.

Peacock and jungle fowl are extremely plentiful the peacocks giving us capital practice with the rifle. We succeeded in bagging a good many.

As my leave was nearly up I had to make my way as quickly as possible through Tjiandjoer and Buitenzorg to Batavia, passing through a very fine country which, unfortunately, from the constant and excessive rains, I was unable to see distinctly.

Soon after my return to Singapore I was ordered to proceed to Labuan, which our Government had lately annexed, and of which Sir James Brooke, the Rajah of Sarawak, was made Governor and Commander in Chief. Thirty European marines had been put ashore as garrison, and as they were being decimated by fever, it was decided to send Sepoys, so I was ordered with eighty men to relieve the marines. Captain Harry Keppel (now Admiral Sir Harry Keppel, G.C.B.) took me over in his fine ship the "Meander." There was no cabin for myself or my subaltern, so a very comfortable canvas one was rigged up between two of the guns on the main deck. My subaltern, a Scotchman, was not a good sailor, and had to confine himself to our cabin. On the second morning he came up on deck with such a serious look on his pale face, that I thought something was gone wrong with the detachment. I had brought with me a Minah Bird which could imitate almost anything, and the only place I had to put it was over the wash-hand stand, to which poor D., deadly seasick, constantly rushed; the bird after a very short time imitated his retching so exactly that it made the poor fellow much worse, and irritated him beyond endurance. He rushed up to me and in broad Scotch said, "I tell you what it is Hamilton, if you don't take that dommed bird away, I'll wring his neck."

The first impression of Labuan was not very cheering, a bit of land covered with high forest trees looming out of mist and rain, and nearly every one down with fever. The Rajah Brooke was very ill with it, and of the thirty marines five had died, twenty were in hospital, and five only fit for duty. The site of the settlement was on a low swampy flat, a miserable looking spot with a few wretched temporary huts. It was arranged that my detachment was not to be located in this feverish place; some ground on a higher level about two and a half miles from the settlement had been partly cleared, and temporary barracks were being prepared; they were to have been ready on our arrival, but were not half finished. For the first day or two I took the detachment on shore during the day and returned to the ship in the evening. There was no landing place, and as my men were in uniform some of the sailors had to carry them "pick-a-back" to the shore. The sailors were up to all kinds of larks. One would stumble forward sending poor Jack Sepoy sprawling into the sea. Another would fall backwards and nearly drown the unfortunate man on his back. I found this would not do, so I remained on shore and packed as many men as I could into the only hut available, and the remainder I put on duty. In a day or two we got things more comfortable, although the men grumbled much, as we had to work in constant rain, which made the ground a muddy swamp; but a Malay pirate had sent me word that he was coming with seven hundred men to cut our throats, and although he never came, I was obliged to be prepared for him.

Whilst making a road to the new barracks, we had a very narrow escape from a serious catastrophe. A number of fine casuarina trees grew round the barracks, these trees have long needle-like spines which fall to the ground in great profusion and cover the surface in some places to the depth of two or three feet, which in wet weather form a spongy swamp, and in dry weather a soft elastic carpet. We happened just at this time to have a spell of very fine hot weather. I took the opportunity to practice the men in ball shooting so as to give a warm reception to the gentleman and his seven hundred men should they come. Some of the burning cartridge paper set fire, without our noticing it, to this dry and spongy carpet of spines, and it increased with such rapidity that very soon the whole plain was in a blaze, and the fire rapidly approached the barracks. Our water supply was soon expended without having made much impression. Fortunately beneath the spines was a layer of fine white sand, and by heaping this on the flames we managed to smother them. At one time, although we had cut trenches in all directions the fire was so close to the barracks that I almost gave up all hope of saving them. Later in the afternoon a fresh danger was reported. The field magazine in which were stored about seventy thousand cartridges was in danger. So I had to move them at once. Where to put them was the question. I was afraid if I placed them with the barrack guard some careless fellow might drop a match or light amongst them, so the only place I could think of was under and around my bed, and there they remained till morning.

The whole interior of the island except where the barracks were placed was one dense forest of enormous trees; there was not much jungle except on the edge of the numerous creeks and ravines. Once having entered the forest you never saw the sky or a ray of sunlight till you came out of it, nothing but a grey gloomy sort of twilight. I never ventured into it without a compass and timing myself and when coming to a sandy ravine making a rough chart, and I was thus able to pilot myself back to the barracks, though more than once I miscalculated and found myself on the sea shore. The best plan, however, was blazing the trees, which obviated much of the difficulty. A ship's captain boasted that he could walk from Coal Point straight down to Victoria (the settlement) through the centre of the island and scorned the idea of taking a compass with him. "He could not lose himself in such a small triangular island only nine miles long by five broad, the idea was too preposterous," so one fine morning away he started; he did not appear at his destination by the next morning, so a search party from the Man-of-War then in the harbour started to find him. After a long time they came upon him thoroughly exhausted. He had found many of the creeks and swamps impassable and in trying to get round them lost his bearings; and being unable to see the sky he appeared to have wandered continually in a circle. In crossing one of these creeks when struggling in the mud he suddenly perceived what he thought was a fallen log but which proved to be a huge alligator calmly eyeing him. He shouted and waved his hat but for some time the brute remained motionless. At last to his immense relief it slowly moved away.

I was much struck with the size and height of some of the camphor trees, the Rajah had two of the largest measured, they were over 300 feet high and the boles could easily have concealed a coach and four.

I have very little to record in the sporting way; although tracks of deer and pig and other game were found quite fresh in many places, it was most difficult to see anything from the density of the forest. On 12th March, 1849, I was out in the swamp at the back of the lines, and was returning home, when I stopped to catch a beautiful butterfly. As I was creeping up to it I heard something move ahead and saw the outline of a very large boar. At first I thought it was a deer. It stood apparently listening about forty yards off; I took a deliberate aim and threw him on his tracks, then reloaded and crept up. As the beast was

THE BIG BOAR OF LABUAN (Sus barbatus).

kicking about and trying to get up I gave him a ball in his head, which however, missed the brain, and did not even stun him, but only made him more savage, so I retreated to reload. When I came up again he was very savage and tried hard to rise and get at me, but this time I put a ball into his brain and effectually settled him, and on going close up I was perfectly astonished at his immense size, and at his most extraordinary head, long and thick with bristles on each side of the face. The height at the shoulder was three feet four inches, length from snout to root of tail six feet three inches, length of head one foot three inches. Now, as the length of a tolerably fine Indian boar is five feet from snout to root of tail, and stands a little over two feet six inches, this fellow was indeed a monster.

On the same morning I saw some curious bees' nests made by a little bee not larger than a house fly. The nests were made of earth, and stuck on the side of a tree, and had long tubes sticking out like the neck of a bottle.

After five months' sojourn in Labuan, I returned to Singapore in April, 1849.

[1] *A Species of Trigonia.*

CHAPTER V.

BEARS.

THEIR SIZE—SAVAGE DISPOSITION—MODE OF GETTING THEIR FAVOURITE FOOD—THE BEAR IN HIS SUMMER HOUSE—MY FIRST BEAR—WHO THE DEUCE ARE YOU ?—DANGER OF APPROACHING A WOUNDED BEAR—THREE BEARS MARKED DOWN—WE TAKE OFF OUR BOOTS—I MISS STOPPING HIM—HE IS UPON ME AT ONCE—A SHARP PINCH—A FUNNY ADVENTURE WITH AN OLD SHE BEAR—I DIDN'T DO IT, MA—THE OLD DOG BEAR AND HIS WIFE—HABITS OF WOUNDED BEARS.

THE Indian black bear (*Ursus labiatus*) the Rich (pronounced Reech) of Southern India is, as Hawkeye says, "a rum customer and dangerous, but amusing and interesting from its queer ways and eccentric habits." He is by some called the sloth bear, but as the above author remarks "the heart of many a sportsman when pursued by a wounded bear, would have rejoiced had his movements partaken of the Genus Sloth." The hair is very black, long and shaggy, the muzzle and tip of the feet of a dull yellowish white with a white V shape mark on the breast. The length of the old males, is, from five to six feet and height about three feet. Hawkeye states that the bears of the Northern Division about Berhampore appear to be of a more savage disposition than the animals down

South, but it will be seen that at times the Southern brutes are savage enough to satisfy any one. Jerdon, in his Mammals of India, quoting from Tickell says, "The power of suction in the bear, as well as of propelling wind from its mouth is very great. It is by these means enabled to procure with ease, its common food of white ants and larvae; on arriving at an ant hill, the bear scrapes away with the fore feet until he reaches the large combs at the bottom of the galleries. It then with violent puffs dissipates the dust and crumbled particles of the nest and sucks out the inhabitants of the comb by such forcible inhalations as to be heard at two hundred yards distance or more. Large larvae are in this way sucked out from great depths under the soil. . . .
"In running the bear moves in a rough canter shaking up and down but gets over very bad ground with great speed, regardless of tumbles down the rough places. The sucking of the paw accompanied by a drumming noise when at rest is common to all bears, especially after meals, and during the heat of the day they may often be heard puffing and humming far down in the caverns or fissures of rocks."

The first bear I killed was in our trip in the Dandilly Forest. He had taken up his abode for the day in the middle of a bamboo clump, the centre stems of which had been cut out by the natives, leaving the outer ones standing, affording a nice shady sort of summer house, and in this the bear was fast asleep. Our shikaries brought us up to the opposite side of the entrance without awaking him; we soon did so, however, by opening a fusilade. He did not attempt to bolt, only tried hard to get at us through the bamboos but in a very short time he was "hors de combat"; it was very like shooting a bear in a cage, but we were young at

TRIED HARD TO GET AT US THROUGH THE BAMBOOS.

the sport and much excited. The only other bear shot on this trip I had the killing of all to myself; I was out with a wild looking village shikarie after deer or anything I could get; suddenly the man whispered "reech, reech" (bear, bear) and was in such a frantic state of excitement that he threw his arms round me and I had some difficulty in throwing him off. I could not see the bear, but we heard him in the dry nullah (water course). He was making such a row that I at first thought there were two of them; I could hear him coming nearer and nearer, when suddenly he appeared and stood up on his hind legs about twenty yards from me with a most comical look of "Who the deuce are you?" Aiming at the centre of the white V across his chest, I fired, and on receiving the shot he began dancing "Jim Crow," but after a minute or two he started off. I soon caught him up, and gave him a couple more shots, but the first had done its work effectually, and after running a short distance he fell over dead. I ran considerable risk in placing myself alongside of a wounded bear in the open, for if he had not been so badly wounded he would have been pretty certain to have come at me.

Some six months after this, I was out on a bear shooting expedition with a brother officer, on some rocky jungly hills about thirty-five miles from our station, where bears were said to abound. The plan adopted in that part of the country was to send people out before daylight, to watch for the bears coming back to the hills after their night's marauding, when they would either retire into some rocky cave or under some thick bush. The first day nothing was done, so we remained in camp, the wonder of the villagers who came in swarms to look at us. The next morning three bears were reported to be marked down, so as soon as we had despatched our breakfast we started off. Our first visit was to a she bear and her three-parts-grown cub; they had been marked down into a large bush, but had afterwards moved into a cave, to the mouth of which we quietly crept, having taken off our boots to make less noise. The village man with us made signs that he could see the bear; I peered in and there she was about ten yards from the entrance of the cave, and as I whispered to my companion, "I can see her, shall I fire?" out she came, full tilt at me; I fired, and my companion followed suit immediately, which turned her a little, and as she passed me, I gave her the other barrel, when she only ran a short distance and laid down under a rock, and as she rose I shot her through the head. We then heard the beaters crying out that there was another bear afoot. My companion got the start of me as I had to load, and when I came up to him I found he had wounded the bear, so I left it to him, and after a long chase over very rocky ground, he killed it. We were pretty well blown, and I felt uncommonly sore about the feet, and on looking down I perceived that I had no boots on. My stockings were all in rags and my feet a good deal cut, but in the excitement I had forgotten all about my boots.

After a rest, we started for number three, and on the way met one of our shikaries, who told us two more bears were marked down—all dog bears, and all in different places. Five bears in one day would be grand. I was, to use an old school phrase, a little bit "too cocky" at having stopped the first bear, and I expressed a hope that No. 3 would be a good fighter; my wish was fulfilled more to the letter than I anticipated.

"HE WAS UPON ME AT ONCE."

After a ride of some three or four miles we arrived at the ground. My companion was posted above and I lower down on a very steep rocky hill side with bushes scattered about. The bear was said to have laid up under a big bush. After some time we heard the beaters yelling frantically and knew the bear was up. Presently I got a glimpse of him and immediately afterwards my companion fired and rolled him over; as he did not get up and all was quiet, I thought he was dead, and left my post, but presently there was another shot and a tremendous yelling from the bear; a noise very like what a stout old gentleman would make on being punched in the ribs—Oh!—Oh!—Oh! As the bear passed an open bit of ground above me I let drive at him; he saw me immediately, and down he came at me with a furious roar. I waited until he was within a few yards when I gave him the other barrel, but as it did not stop him I thought it was high time to cut and run; in turning to do so I tripped over a rock and fell flat on my face. He was upon me at once, and looking over my shoulder I saw into the bear's mouth as he made a grab at my head. It was an awful moment. By a desperate struggle I slid away from him, but he pinned me by the thigh; oh, what a pinch it was. I hit him about the nose and face as hard as I could with my fists, my gun having fallen out of my reach, and luckily for me, as a bear cannot stand a blow on the nose, he let go. I gave him no time to get hold of me again, and I found myself some sixty yards up the hill I don't know how! Both the men with me, though armed, had bolted. My companion seeing the bear on the top of me came hastening down, met the brute and shot him. He was much surprised on calling out for me to hear my voice so far up the hill side. I came down not feeling a bit the worse for my adventure. My friend at first thought my face was torn, but it proved to be nothing but the blood of the bear as he tried to seize me by the head. There were four holes in my trousers, but no signs of blood, and as I felt no pain I fancied I had escaped with only a pinch, and we had rather a hot dispute as to whether my last shot had hit him. We eventually started for number four, but had not gone far when I began to feel very queer and faint; I got some water which refreshed me and we started again, but feeling very uncomfortable about the hip, I thought I might as well see if I was bitten. My friend said on my doing so he saw my jaw drop on to my chest. My thigh bone was quite exposed, so taking all things into consideration, and the bears being a good way off, I thought it best to make for our camp. We managed to rig up a native bed—for I was now so stiff I could not move without great pain, and by travelling through the night I arrived at my house without further mishap, and in a month was able to get about. I must however allow that I was not quite so steady the next time I was posted for a bear, but the nervousness, we should have called it by another name in those days, soon wore off, and I saw many a bear afterwards bite the dust to my rifle.

On another occasion I had a funny adventure with a bear, I had turned out soon after 7 a.m. On going over the hill, I heard a rush and a roar to my right and saw some large animal trotting away. Atley whispered, "It's a tiger," so I was rather careful how I advanced as I could hear it growling a little way on. However, as soon as we got on the tracks we saw it was a bear, so away we went after it; the moist jungle showing a fine broad track which we followed for a long distance. At last just ahead I heard the peculiar blow through the mouth which a bear makes; stepping lightly forward we came to more open ground, when Atley pointed to an old bear and cub crossing about forty yards above us. I waited for the old lady to pass a tree, but at that moment I think she must have winded me, for with a sudden exclamation of alarm, she sat up, turning round towards us, her body being partly hidden by the tree, but as there

"I DIDN'T DO IT, MA!"

was no time to be lost, I at once fired. On receiving the shot, with a ferocious roar she rushed upon the youngster, and how she did pitch into it. The little brute kept screaming out as if it said, "I didn't do it, Ma": after a bit it got away, and as she turned round, I gave her another shot which rolled her over; a very old she bear with all her teeth quite worn down.

Another bear adventure is worth recording. One day when out from the hut I spied two bears on the long sloping hill which leads down to the Crags; I had a long and exciting stalk down to them, and got to the edge of the shola on the hill above which they were feeding about 150 yards away; I could not get closer to them, so I stood watching them from behind a tree for a long time hoping they would approach nearer. How busy they were, turning up the stones for ants and digging under the tufts of grass for grubs—so comical in all their movements—evidently an old dog bear and his wife. After waiting until my patience was nearly exhausted and the sun nearly setting, we decided to go round the hill and get above them. We soon got round and I was pleased to find the wind blowing strong in our faces as we crept up the hill; on looking over the crest there was the back of Mr. B. not forty yards from us, a step forward exposed the whole of his broadside. He was busy digging, and a little below him, there was Mrs. B. looking hard at me. There was not a moment to lose, so with a steady aim, I planted a projectile behind his shoulder. He jumped up into the air, bit at the wound, and then rushed furiously at Mrs. B., she like a proper spirited female immediately resented such untoward treatment, and the row the two made as they tumbled over one another was something tremendous. I took a pot shot at the black mass as it rolled about, but the rifle missed fire, the report of the cap, however, made them look up, they separated, and bolted. I ran down the hill after them and put another ball into Mr. B. as he stood up for an instant with his back towards me. His progress down the hill was now most absurd, all the time singing out lustily, and after running for a few paces, deliberately tumbling head over heels, again running three or four paces and another somersault, and so on. Mrs. B. who had got on some little distance in front turned back and came up the hill again, whether to charge me or assist her spouse I know not, but his extraordinary method of coming down the hill appeared so to astonish her that she turned tail and rushed into the shola. I waited for him to stop and give me a fairer shot than the round ball he was making of himself, but he would not, so I fired just as he entered the shola. Francis said I hit him, but I doubt it, as his mode of entering the shola was so absurd that I was unsteady from laughing. Instead of going nose first as a bear ought to do, he entered head over heels exactly as the harlequin at a pantomime would disappear through the wall of a house. As soon as he got well into the wood he sat down and began roaring most piteously, every roar being answered by a large black monkey. As it was getting dark we had not time to make much of a search so we gave it up. Francis was quite certain that we should find him in the morning, but we did not and never saw him again.

It seems to be a peculiarity with bears, at any rate with the Indian bear, that they must always bite something when they are wounded. One day I was out looking for a tiger when I came across an old bear sitting up busily scratching herself. I stalked close up to her (a little over twenty yards), by which time she had commenced feeding again, so I waited till she turned towards me when I dropped her with a ball between the shoulders. However, up she got, and began singing out most lustily, so I gave her another which broke her fore leg, when she instantly seized and crushed it to pieces, I could hear the bones breaking.

A third shot finished the savage old brute. She was a very handsome and very large female, measuring six feet two inches as she lay. Another day I knocked over an old she bear on her tracks, but before she gave up the ghost she got one of her fore paws in her mouth, her fangs nearly meeting in the foot.

I COULD HEAR THE BONES BREAKING.

THE IBEX (The Neilgherry Wild Goat):
MALE AND FEMALE.

CHAPTER VI.

IBEX SHOOTING ON THE NEILGHERRIES, ANNAMULLIES, AND PULNIES.

EXCURSION TO THE SEVEN PAGODAS—SPORTING TRIP TO DAVAROY-DROOG—MISERABLE SPORT—ATTACKED BY FEVER—MEDICAL BOARD—SENT TO THE HILLS—ARRIVAL AT OOTY—FIRST IMPRESSIONS—FIRST INTRODUCTION TO IBEX—THE OLD SADDLE BACKS—EXCITING STALKS—MAGNIFICENT SCENERY—HABITS OF THE IBEX—ITS ENEMIES—CHARMS AND ATTRACTIONS OF THE PURSUIT OF IBEX—MY FIRST IBEX—TIGER (THE DOG) AND THE WOUNDED IBEX—MALLOCK'S BUNGALOW—MICHAEL'S LUCK—A CLOSE SHAVE—I GO HOME "KOOSH" THE OLD BUCK OF KUDAKARNAL—THE GRAND OLD SADDLE BACK—THE THREE LEGGED BUCK I DID NOT GET.

IN June, 1849, I went to England and did not return to Madras till November, 1852. In the following year I made an excursion to the Seven Pagodas, a curious sort of place like the Tunbridge Wells rocks magnified; some of them having been formed into beautiful temples covered with carvings of figures, of men and animals, &c., very well executed.

I especially noticed two monkeys, one fleaing the other, cut out of the hard stone, also two elephants with a man seated, and in another temple, the figure of a man milking a buffalo whilst she licks her calf, evidently by the same hand which carved the elephants. Some of the temples formed by detached masses of stone were very beautiful, especially one with four columns of great height, which was most elegant in shape.

In September, 1853, I went on a trip to Bidaree, about twenty-six miles from Bangalore, and began again my sporting days, first by sitting up all night for a tiger which would not come, and in the day time looking for bears which were not at home; or away over the hills as a last hope of meeting some sort of game; but not a thing did I see.

On the 5th October, in the same year, I started with Sweet and Digby for a trip to Davaroy-droog, and a more miserable ten days' sport I never had. The only result was that I and both my companions caught very bad fevers. Digby was taken ill a day or two before me, and Sweet on the same day; my attack was very severe, in fact it rested on the turn of a hair whether I was to live or die. Thank God! the turn was on the side of life; but who would have thought that we should have got fever at Davaroy-droog, as it was supposed to be quite safe. On the 30th of November I went up with Sweet before the Medical Board, and we were ordered to the hills till the end of March, with extension of leave if necessary. We left Bangalore on 12th December, arriving at Ootacamund at sunset on the 15th. The first view of the place was not very picturesque, and very un-Indian; my first impression was that I should not like it, but this soon changed. Next day I was up and out soon after sunrise, found the ground covered with white hoar frost, and the air delightfully cool and invigorating, and I was much surprised to meet several rosy cheeked children.

It was when on the Nielgherries that I first saw an ibex, and was introduced to certainly one of the most pleasant as well as most exciting sports of Southern India. I cannot do better than quote what Hawkeye says about this animal and its pursuit. "The Nielgherry wild goat (*Hemitragus hylocrius*)[1] as styled by Jerdon, though I think mountain goat a more appropriate term, is a species of the genus Capra, distinctive to Southern India, the only other kind of goat approaching in likeness to it being the Tahr of the Himalayas (*Hemitragus-jemlaicus*). Our mountain goat is a sturdy, I may almost say, a massively formed animal, with short legs, and remarkably strong fetlocks, a heavy carcase, short and well ribbed up; combining strength and agility, wonderful to behold; their habits are gregarious, and the does are seldom met with separate from the flock or herd, though males often are; the latter are considerably larger than the females and as they grow old assume a peculiar distinctive appearance, the hair of the back becoming lighter, almost white in some instances, while that on the flank darkens, causing what is called a saddle to appear, and from that time they become known to shikaries as the *Saddle back* of the herd, an object of ambition in the eyes of the true sportsman."

---

[1] *Capra warryato, Gray.* The term *warryato* being composed of two tamul words, *wurrai* a precipice, and *ádú* a goat.

"It is a pleasant sight to watch a herd of ibex when undisturbed, the kids frisking here and there on pinnacles or ledges of rocks and beetling cliffs where there seems scarcely safe foothold for anything much larger than a grass-hopper, the old mother looking calmly on. Then again, see the caution observed in taking up their resting or abiding places for the day, where they may be warmed by the sun, listening to the roar of many waters, figuratively we may say, chewing the cud of contentment and giving themselves up to the full enjoyment of their nomadic life and its romantic haunts. Usually before reposing, one of the herd, generally an old doe, may be observed intently gazing below, apparently scanning every spot in the range of her vision, sometimes for half an hour or more, before she is satisfied that 'all is well,' but strange to say seldom or never looking up to the rocks above. Then being satisfied on the one side, she follows the same process on the other, eventually calmly lying down contented with the precautions she has taken. Her post as sentinel is generally a prominent one on the edge or corner of some ledge, well sheltered from the wind and warmed by the sun, along which the herd dispose themselves as inclined, fully trusting in the watchful guardian whose manœuvres I have been describing; should the sentinel be joined by another, or her kid come and lie down by her, they invariably place themselves back to back, or in such a manner that they can keep a good look out on either side. A solitary male goes through all this by himself, and wonderfully careful he is, but when with the herd he reposes in security, leaving it to the females to take precautions for their mutual safety.

"Although so wary in their habits, these animals are at

times not so difficult to stalk as the sambur; with the wind favourable, they can usually be easily approached from above; their conduct also when suddenly alarmed by the crack of a rifle is curious; instead of a steady or direct flight as when they see or smell their enemy, they start about from rock to rock in a bewildered manner, at times squatting like hares, then springing up with a shrill whistle, hesitating for a moment which line to take, all the time affording opportunities for the sportsman to pick and choose his shots."

"Besides their enemy man, they have a very wily poacher to guard against, viz., the leopard; wherever ibex are found, there assuredly will the marks of this their stealthy foe be detected. From the very strong scent emitted by the ibex, especially the males, the leopard has no difficulty in finding its prey, and I believe many fall victims to its rapacious maw.

"To my mind the pursuit of the ibex is more exciting if possible, than that of the stag. The peril that attends the adventurer on the crags and fearful precipices, where the quarry resort, the grand and sublime scenery, the giddy heights and sombre depths, the danger and difficulty of the stalk, all combine in adding to the charms and attractions of the pursuit, and make a man feel proud of his success when he has brought to bag a fine old saddle back."

The ibex generally go in herds from six to ten, but at times they are found in much greater numbers. On the 20th April, 1854, when creeping over the crest of a hill in Michael's Valley, on the Annamullies, I found myself suddenly in the midst of at least sixty, and at another time I came upon a herd of twenty-seven. Both these herds were extremely wild, which was accounted for from their having been lately harassed by hill men, the Moodowas, who had constructed across one of their runs, a barrier of stout bushes, forming a strong hedge, with weak places ten or twelve feet apart; across which a strong running noose was firmly secured. The ibex were then driven up to these barriers and were ruthlessly snared and shot.

Jerdon's description of this animal is as follows:—"The adult male is a dark sepia brown, with a pale reddish brown saddle more or less marked, and paler brown on the sides and beneath. Legs somewhat grizzled with white, dark brown in front, and paler posteriorly. The head is dark, grizzled with yellowish brown, and the eye is surrounded by a pale fawn-coloured ring. Horns short, much curved, nearly in contact at the base, gradually diverging, strongly keeled internally, round externally, with numerous close rings not so prominent as in the Tahr. There is a large callous spot on the knees surrounded by a fringe of hair, and the male has a short stiff mane on the neck and withers. The hair is short, thick and coarse."[1]

It was on the 6th of March, 1854 that I killed my first ibex. I had gone on the 2nd with Brine to an old ruined Tappu Station between the Avalanche and Sispara. We walked the last fourteen miles to get ourselves in trim. On arriving, I found my tent already pitched and all very comfortable. The next morning, the 3rd, we were out by six o'clock and went over a mountain where Brine a short time

---

[1] Mr. Lydeker, in an article in the *Field* newspaper of March 19th, 1892, states that the Nielgherry ibex has a beard, which forms another point of distinction between the Wariatu and the Tahr. This appears to be a mistake, as the ibex of the Nielgherries has no beard.—Ed.

THE IBEX HILLS, ANNAMULLIES.

before had seen from forty to fifty ibex and had shot five. We did not see one, so bivouacked under a tree for breakfast and waited till it was time to watch for sambur, meanwhile I amused myself drawing ibex and deer on the barkless trunk of an old tree. Nothing appearing and being a very long distance from home, we proceeded by the side of a splendid forest stretching the whole extent of a long valley, and continuing down to the low country; in crossing a little branch shola, a large sambur jumped up in front of the shikarie who got frantically excited, and on his pointing out to me the stag standing broadside on, not above fifty yards off, I took what I thought was a very cool pot, but somehow or other managed to send the ball just over his back. I was awfully disgusted at the miss, particularly as a little farther on a jungle cock flew up into a tree and I knocked him over with a ball through his body. A few minutes afterwards I saw a hind standing breast on looking at me about eighty yards off; I could only see her neck and half her chest, but being determined if possible to retrieve my former wretched shot I took a steady aim, put a ball in the centre of the lower part of her neck, and another from the second barrel into the back of her neck as she dashed away, and I found her stone dead a short way in the jungle.

On the 6th we were out soon after eight a.m., to stalk the ground on the right of the road to Sispara, in hopes of finding ibex; we had some splendid views of the jungle, hills and precipices on our right, and halted for breakfast at ten, without having seen a single animal. The ibex hill we intended searching was covered with mist so we started for another hill on our left. Brine was rather seedy, preferring to remain quiet, so I went up alone and soon came on plenty of marks and the shikarie declared he could smell the ibex. Presently he stopped and pointed; I took a step forward and saw a doe ibex feeding about sixty yards below; as she turned and exposed her side, I fired, saw the ball strike and I gave her the contents of the other barrel as she dashed away, but soon she fell over and in her struggles rolled down a precipice full eighty feet in height; I found her quite dead at the bottom, a fine beast with good horns. After cutting off her head I went down to Brine who was waiting for us below, and after stopping there some time proceeded to watch for sambur, the shikaries going up to the top of a high hill. We had not waited long when we saw three ibex come over a hill some distance away; one a large buck standing on the sky line looking out. As soon as they had all disappeared I started to stalk them with Brine's shikarie, who had come down from the hill, but they had not waited for us.

MY FIRST IBEX.

Meanwhile Brine had moved from where we had left him and we saw him stalking four ibex, all apparently very large bucks; however, it turned out that he had not seen these large ones, but only the outward sentinel above, a female, which he stalked to within sixteen paces and put a ball through her head; she rolled over and over down the hill, the remainder of the herd, nine in number dashing away, his second bullet scattering the dust over some of them; they came along the rocks over which I had been stalking and by running round under the shoulder of the hill I crept over the top just as they were all passing some seventy yards below me; I fired at the biggest looking buck at the moment he had caught sight of me, heard the ball strike him and then fired the other barrel at another large fellow as he went away, but missed him. I immediately took the light rifle, fired again at him, and hearing the hit distinctly, I fired the second barrel at a third buck as he dashed up the opposite spur of the hill, but the ball struck close along side of him. The shikarie said if any were hit I should find them lying down further on, as a wounded ibex never goes far; sure enough a few yards further on I saw him lying on a rock; he got up before I could shoot and ran into a shola close at hand, a sure sign of being hard hit, as ibex never enter the woods if they can help it.

As soon as Brine came up we had a search for him, but it being sunset and getting dark we gave it up and turned homewards, intending to look for him on the morrow. The next morning we started a little before eight with all the coolies and Brine's three dogs to look in the shola for my wounded ibex. After beating for some time we heard his dog Tiger baying at something; from the noise we thought it must be a bear or a tiger, but in about five minutes out rushed the ibex with the dog after him. Brine fired but the ball passed in and out of the skin on the back without injuring the spine. As soon as he got to the top of the hill he turned to bay, rearing and butting at the dog like an old billy goat and keeping Mr. Tiger at a very respectable distance. I ran up the hill and put a ball into him, but it did not stop him; again and again he came to bay, when another ball through the shoulders rolled him over and over down the hill: a noble animal of immense size; he was thirty-nine and a half inches (three feet three and a half inches) at the shoulder; my shot yesterday had struck him too far back, his horns were rather stumpy from age. He was a very black old saddle back.

In July, 1854, I bought Mallock's Bungalow for 200 rupees.[1] In June, in the following year, I was out there with Michael, and one day on returning from ibex shooting when passing through a shola we came upon the fresh track of a cheeta or tiger. We pushed on, and Michael, who was a few yards in front of me, put up his rifle and fired. I saw something brown dash on and asked—"Was that a cheeta?"

THE HUT, PYKARA.

"No," he cried, "A royal tiger." He had not his own rifle, but a short stocked one of Clogston's, and in following the

[1] This is the famous Hut at Pykara, where for many a year he had the pleasure of entertaining and showing sport to so many of his friends; amongst them the late Prince Frederick of Schleswig Holstein, the late Sir Victor Brooke, Bob Jago, and the oldest and most intimate of all, General Michael. The hut was still in his possession at his decease. —ED.

tiger up we found that he had missed him. Though he has knocked over so many elephants and constantly been in jungles full of tigers, this was the first shot he ever had at one. Two days after, Clogston, another famous elephant shot, who was also with us, fell in with a tiger lying down, and stalked him to within seventy yards. He took a steady shot and struck him so severely, that the hind quarters appeared to be paralysed, but he crawled away and C. wisely did not follow him; he described the fury of the beast, when hit, as very grand. It is the first he also ever had a shot at: curious that two great elephant hunters should be out here together, and both have their first shots at tigers within three days.

But to return to our ibex. One day in June, 1856, I had an exciting but unsuccessful stalk after a grand old saddle back; while waiting for the mist to clear, as we had seen quite fresh tracks, I sat down; suddenly in a rift of the mist, I saw an old black ibex moving along the hill in the direction of a bluff rock. I was up and after him at once; he kept steadily on, and though once or twice I got within 140 yards, I would not risk the shot. He certainly was a splendid old fellow, his saddle and neck looking quite white. I was most anxious to get him, and that made me lose him, for just as we got to the top of a steep hill and I expected to catch sight of him some distance beyond, I saw him much nearer, and creeping forward I got within seventy yards of him: he was standing stern on. Instead of waiting, as I ought to have done, for him to turn, I stepped to one side to get a better shot, he saw me at once, and dashed on some twenty paces, and then stood broad side-on, such a nice shot; but I was too hurried, and being rather blown, missed him clean. I ran forward and saw him standing at the corner of a rock but I was too late; as I pulled the trigger he disappeared and I heard the ball strike the rock, and there was an end of it.

THE OLD SADDLE-BACK.

One morning in October, 1856, I went with Michael to Codaka-Mullay, a well-known ibex hill; we had to take a rope to help us to scale the almost perpendicular precipices so as to reach the upper plateau. At one part we were stopped by a ledge which overhung the rock, but working round and with the help of the rope, we eventually gained the plateau. We soon came upon the tracks of our game, and at the further end we saw an ibex lying down on some rocks. I think he saw us, but as he did not appear to be alarmed, Michael slid down under cover of the grass till he got within a hundred yards—his ball struck just too low.

The moment he fired I ran as hard as I could over the hill and came upon the ibex standing broadside on, about seventy yards off, fired, and down he fell on his side. As I ran up a small kid crossed my path, and as we wanted meat I shot it, at the report the wounded ibex jumped up at my feet; I fired again and missed it, and it ran into some dense bushes overhanging a fearful precipice. I crept down after it and while so occupied heard Michael fire; I thought he had fallen in with my wounded one, but found on returning that he had killed a fine buck. It happened thus: the heat being very great, he (Michael) had laid down under a tree, but seeing a fresh track close to him in some bushes, told Atley, his shikarie, to see what it was, and got up to be ready, when out rushed a buck ibex; he put both balls into him, and finished him off with another, killing him close to the edge of a precipice, over which, had he fallen, he would never have been seen again.

We decided on having tiffin under a projecting rock affording a wild and magnificent view, and sent Atley to look for my wounded beast and shoot it; giving him my light rifle, but taking off one of the caps for fear of accident. We heard a shot far down below us and after a considerable time, up came our other man, who had been sent back some couple of thousand feet up the mountain for another cap. After giving him what was necessary, away he went down the precipitous side where I should have thought even an ibex could not have gone, and we soon heard another shot. In due time they returned; Atley had killed one, whether mine or not he was unable to say, it had fallen down a precipice where even he could not get at it.

One day when out stalking sambur I came upon a herd of

ibex nine in number with one fine large black fellow amongst them. The old buck soon laid down amongst his wives, a small brown buck going higher up the hill as a sentinel. After carefully surveying the ground he also laid down, we then had to make a long circuit to get at them, it being very doubtful whether I could out-manœuvre the sentinel. The wind being all right, I took off my shoes when I got to the top of the hill and crept cautiously along; presently the heads of some of the does appeared below me, they were up and alarmed not at me but at some coolies who were passing along a road below; it was some time before I could make out the black buck. At last I saw him, still lying down, took a steady shot at him, the ball caught him just behind the withers and he never rose. He was a magnificent old saddle back. The height at the shoulder forty-two inches, circumference of fore arm twelve inches, from the point of the nose to end of tail fifty and a half inches, chest to tail thirty-eight and a quarter inches, nose to root of horn twelve and a half inches. The scenery where I killed him was wild and magnificent in the extreme.

Ibex are very quick of hearing and from the number of loose stones about, one has to be very careful, and I was often obliged to take off my shoes when stalking them. When at the hut on June 12th, 1857, I was off by daylight to the lower crags, but found nothing, and the wind changing I went to the end of the big crag shola so as to meet the wind, sending Francis, my shikarie, to look over the ground lower down. A little higher up I saw a black buck with a doe. I watched them for a short time, and as I could not see Francis, started for the stalk; taking off my shoes when near the spot. The broken ground was beautiful for stalking and I was able to get within thirty-five yards of them. They were both lying down. Just as I raised my rifle the buck looked up and saw me, but it was too late, for the next second a ball from the big rifle was crashing through his

I TAKE OFF MY SHOES.

shoulder. They were up in a moment and disappeared down the rock but I knew the saddle back was done for. I ran on to the edge and saw him below me on his side, giving his last kick, the doe standing near him, but before I could pull the trigger she was off; I waited for her to stop at a rock, and as she did so, I fired and heard the tell, but she dashed on as if unhurt. I saw her farther down staggering by the edge of a precipice, and after one or two struggles to keep her feet, over she went clean down into the valley below. I whistled nearly all the wind out of me for Francis, as a thick mist covering everything was coming up; at last he came and

I trudged home "koosh," leaving the men to skin the ibex and bring in what meat they wanted.

One or two more extracts from my journal and I think I shall have said enough about ibex shooting. But the sport is so exciting, and at the same time, being carried on amongst the highest mountains, and amidst such magnificent scenery, so exhilarating, that I may be pardoned for dwelling so much upon it.

I was out very early one morning, when I came suddenly upon a doe ibex and a half grown kid; not wishing to disturb them, I crept back to Francis and we agreed to look just beyond them and see if there was a buck. As I craned over the rock I saw a large brown buck looking at me about sixty yards off, his hind quarters hidden by a rock; I fired, heard the tell, ran on and saw the herd, consisting of a dozen or more, galloping down the side or the slope about a hundred and forty yards away; after going a short distance they stood bewildered, when I again fired and hit a doe; as I was following her, out bolted the brown buck from a hollow; he ran about two hundred yards and then sat down on his haunches, presently sinking on his side; there were two small bucks on the rocks above him, and the old fellow, after looking at them for some time, to my astonishment jumped up, disappeared behind some rocks, and was out of sight by the time I had got up to where he had been lying. I followed the wounded doe until her tracks disappeared over a most frightful precipice, which was quite impossible to descend, so I had to give her up. I hate leaving a wounded animal, but there was no help for it. As I returned up the hill I thought to myself, "Well, this is neat, I shall lose them both, but not without another try;" so away I went to hunt up the tracks of the buck; I took them up where it had laid down and followed them along the side of the hill to the rocks, beyond which we lost all trace; but while hunting in the only direction he could

A CLOSE SHAVE.

have taken, a rocky slope with bushes overhanging a fearful precipice, I saw Francis, who was some distance from me and near the edge, give a sudden start, look behind him, and then make signs to me to come quick. Come quick, indeed, over such ground! Picking my way carefully I got up to him at last, he pointed, and there was the ibex lying on a rock below me. I planted a ball just behind the shoulder and he fell over on his side, but in the death struggles he rolled off the rock, and in another minute would have tumbled over the precipice into the jungles far below, had not the horns caught fast in the bough of a rhododendron bush. The hind legs were within a yard of the precipice, and a tremendous one it was, if I may judge from the sound of the fall when we tumbled the body over after securing the head. It was indeed a close shave of losing him. We had a rough scramble to get down to him, but a worse one to get back. I was quite in a tremble for fear that Francis would be pulled over by the weight of the ibex when he unhooked him from the bush. He was a fine old saddle back with good horns.

There was a well-known old saddle back which frequented the rocks about Kodakarnal, whose head and horns it was my ambition to add to my trophies. I had many a stalk after him, but he always managed to give me the slip. One evening when busy drawing, the boy who I had stationed at the look-out, came running in to say that the saddle back was in sight. I started off at once, and when I got to the station, on putting up the glasses, there, sure enough, was my old friend. He was busy at his evening meal, keeping a sharp look-out, and close to the edge of a precipice, which, with an occasional break of slope and rock, went clean down to the low country.

The difficulty was to get down to him without being seen; fortunately the wind was all right, and the mist, which

I have so often abused, did me good service now, enabling me to get down the steep slope and under the cover of an intervening spur without disturbing the ibex. With both barrels of my old Ross on full cock I noiselessly mounted the ridge, and as I craned over it, almost at my feet I saw his horns and then his head. I moved half a step forward to uncover his body, but he saw me and was down out of sight in a second. I dashed forward and saw him making tracks some thirty yards below me. I was just going to fire, when he pulled up for a moment, and then I pulled the trigger and a bullet from the true and faithful old rifle went crashing through his shoulders; he tried to dash away, but toppled over a rocky precipice and disappeared in the mist. But where? Fortunately there was a long slope before coming to the final precipice, but so very steep that he could scarcely have stopped there unless the lemon grass and fern, which is very thick, had held him. Peering through the mist we could make nothing of it, but when it cleared a little, I could see his track for some distance down. As there was plenty of grass to hold on by, we cautiously descended, and at the bottom of the slope there he was, stone dead.

Thus died, as I supposed, the old saddle back of Kodakarnal! Daniel (the boy) says he has known him for eight years, and "no gentleman never could shoot him." We brought up his head, though I did not half like the scramble up the steep wet slope with my rifle in one hand, for a slip backwards would have caused me to reach the low country sooner and quicker than I ever intended.

The boys next day went down and brought home the skin and meat. To my great disappointment Daniel declared that the buck I killed was after all not the black buck of Kodakarnal; that he had seen the Simon Pure on the rocks below, whilst they were skinning the dead ibex, and that he has a white patch on his back "same like cloth put there," and my cook corroborates this. The one I killed has a fine dark brown almost black skin with a grey saddle, horns thirteen inches long, and eight and a half round the base—not a bad buck.

On the 19th of June, 1862, when shooting on the Pulnies, I killed the finest old saddle back that ever fell to my rifle. I was out after Sambur when I saw a fine old buck ibex lying on a rock under a tree, so I set to work to stalk him. To avoid making any noise I took off my shoes, but I found he had moved from where I had last seen him, and as I crept slowly and cautiously along the edge of the slope, I caught sight of him about fifty or sixty yards below me. I could not see his legs, and I was not certain whether he was standing up or lying down. He was broadside on; aiming low with the left barrel of my Laing I fired and heard the tell, saw him stagger and try to recover himself and then fall over; in his death struggles he rolled fifty or sixty yards further down, but his horns catching in a strong tuft of grass, stopped him from going right down into the low country. He was a magnificent old fellow. I could not make him more than forty inches at the shoulder, fair measurement. Shakespear in his book says that some have reached fifty inches, but I think he must have been misinformed.

I will finish my ibex sport with the stalk after the three-legged buck at Naadgany. I will just notice that the crows here seem very fond of settling upon animals. An old crow flew on an ibex I was stalking, and perching on its back probably told it of the threatened danger, as it suddenly ceased feeding and walked off, and the other evening a crow settled on one of the horns of a Sambur I was watching.

On Saturday, 3rd March, 1870, I was up at dawn and went to the Big Hill ibex ground to sketch; having fixed on a spot, I set to work sending Francis to look out, he presently came back and reported a herd of fifteen ibex on Big Hill; he said that there was a buck amongst them very lame, so I went up to have a look, and there was a buck hobbling along on three legs; from the shadows I could not tell whether he was a saddle back, so I started for a stalk and if possible to bag the lame chap. We dodged round behind an opposite hill where we could get a good view, without disturbing them; six of the herd were busy feeding, and for a long time I could not see the others, at last I spied them under a solitary tree, and there amongst them was a saddle back. I made sure he was the lame party and pretty sure he was the one I had wounded at Christmas; the only thing that bothered me was that he appeared to have only one horn, still I might not have noticed this defect on a former occasion. He was beautifully situated for a stalk, so I put on my goloshes; whilst watching him, a doe came up and lay down alongside of him. I was afraid she would spoil my stalk, but the undulation of the ground enabled me to approach within a few yards, and when I raised my head there was the doe on the rock above looking out, but I was able to keep a tuft of scrub between her head and mine. I craned over to look for the buck, but he was not where we had last seen him; a step forward and the doe was off the rock and I saw the saddle back making tracks with the rest about forty yards off. I fired my first barrel without effect, but took a steadier aim with the other and gave him a regular staggerer, however, he held on over the hill. Hastening after him, I came upon the herd, but there was no saddle back with them; Francis called out "There's the big one—shoot." He was under a rock close to me, I saw his head and was going to plug him in the ear, when he moved and I knocked him over with a body shot; to my disappointment he was not the lame buck, and had only one horn; and when they were skinning him I went to the further ridge, but could see nothing. Three days after I went to finish my sketch, and whilst doing so, Francis reported a herd of thirteen ibex with the lame buck amongst them. They were on some rocks on Big Hill slope, beautifully situated for a stalk, so after finishing my drawing, we worked round the opposite hill and reconnoitred them, but, unfortunately a doe popped her head up over the ridge and saw us. Presently the whole herd moved up the hill, so I had to get above them, and on looking over saw them below gradually coming up towards me. Unluckily a young doe caught sight of the top of my topee, and commenced whistling, and as they separated I caught sight of the lame buck between two does about eighty yards away, I took as I thought a steady aim at him, but there was no thud. They were out of sight in a moment, and on dashing forward down the steep hill, I tripped up and fell clean on my forehead and nose which nearly stunned me. As I scrambled up I was only just in time to see the herd careering away down below, the three-legged buck keeping well up with them. He appeared to have but one foreleg, with a lump where the other leg ought to have been. I should have liked very much to have bagged him and seen whether he was born without a leg, or whether it had rotted off, but I never saw him again. It was a bad miss. The wind was blowing strong; I was perhaps too eager, still it was a bad miss, turn it and twist it how I would.

THE IBEX STALKER.

CHAPTER VII.

ELEPHANTS.

THE INDIAN ELEPHANT—IN CAPTIVITY—THEIR INTELLIGENCE AND SAGACITY—THEIR SUNDAY'S PUDDINGS—CONSTITUTION CHANGES BY DOMESTICATION—ELEPHANTS IN THEIR WILD STATE—THEIR POWER OF SCENT—WONDERFUL EXAMPLES OF ENGINEERING—THEIR SIZE—CAUTION WHEN STALKING THEM—MY FIRST TUSKER—THE TUSKER WITHOUT A TAIL—AN AMUSING INCIDENT—ELEPHANT AND BISON—COMING ON A HERD AND THE RESULT—CAPTURE OF A YOUNGSTER—THE TABLES TURNED—HEELS OVER HEAD—A STRANGE SHOT—LAST TRIP AFTER ELEPHANTS—THE GREAT TUSKER OF HASSANOOR—HIS DEATH—MY LAST ELEPHANT—BROOKE STOPS THE CHARGE.

AT one time during my service I had a good deal to do with the Indian elephant, both wild and in captivity. I was in charge of one of the large teak forests in Southern India—the Annamullies—where the wild elephant roamed at will. I had a number of tame elephants employed to drag timber to the stacks. In those days before iron had taken the place of wood, a great deal of teak wood was used in ship building, and this I had to supply to the Bombay Dock Yard. The teak wood is cut into large beams or planks as they are called in the forest, averaging about twenty-six feet in length, and from twelve to fourteen inches square throughout—not a very heavy load for an elephant to drag. A hole is cut at one end of the beam and a thick drag rope is tied to it; this the elephant takes in his mouth, dragging the beam alongside; occasionally a fallen tree lies across the path, and I have often watched with astonishment the wonderful sagacity and intelligence of the animal when such a thing as this occurs. The elephant, the instant the beam touches the obstacle, does not put a particle of pressure on, but calmly steps back, lifts the end on to the fallen tree with his trunk, and then pulls it gently over.[1] Besides dragging the beams to the stack yard the elephants also pile them one over the other with the utmost regularity; no man could do it better. When the logs have been brought to the stack where they are to be piled, the drag rope has to be untied, and it is necessary that a man should accompany the elephant for this purpose, but I had a clever little elephant who untied the drag rope herself, and thus saved the wages of one man the whole time I was in the forest.

An elephant is generally guided and kept in order by a Mahout or keeper, armed with an iron hook and spike which acts as both rein and spear; but in the very damp climate of the Annamullies, the slight scratches and punctures made by

---

[1] The Author evidently does not share the views of Sanderson and others as to the intelligence of this animal. Sanderson in his work (Thirteen years amongst the wild beasts of India) says: "The opinion is generally held by those who have the best opportunity of observing the elephant, that the popular estimate of its intelligence is a greatly exaggerated one, that instead of being the exceptionally wise animal it is believed to be, its sagacity is of a very mediocre description." Sanderson thinks a Newfoundland dog is a much more intelligent creature than an elephant. Blandford takes the same view; he says, "I quite agree with Sanderson in believing that the intelligence of elephants has been greatly overrated; they are singularly docile and obedient; no other animal is known to be capable of domestication when adult to nearly the same extent, and docility in animals is generally, I think, confounded with intelligence."—Ed.

this instrument had a tendency to fester, so we only allowed a light bamboo cane to be used, not thicker than one's little finger, and this answered perfectly. Few people are aware that the elephant with a skin nearly an inch in thickness is one of the most sensitive of animals, and will be as much annoyed or even more so by the sting of a mosquito than by a prod from the Mahout. A blow from a bamboo switch will make an elephant roar out much louder than a school boy does when he has to hold out his hand for punishment. Now by this little bamboo switch the elephants were maintained in perfect order. The Mahout if he had to leave the elephant for a time in the forest would take the animal up to a fallen tree and make him put one forefoot on it, and the bamboo stick would then be balanced on that foot. I have often passed an elephant standing perfectly still with one foot on a fallen tree balancing the stick, and half an hour after found him still in the same position, though the jungle around was teeming with all kinds of elephant luxuries—a wonderful instance of obedience and docility quite apart from their intelligence.

Some of the best working elephants I had were those that had been captured when full grown, yet these, and in fact all tame elephants, have a great dread of the wild ones. On Sundays we used to let all the tame elephants loose, and they had a day to themselves in the forest. They were quite unfettered except by a chain attached to one of the hind legs, and they have often come rushing into the station alarmed by the presence of wild ones in the neighbourhood. There was no fear of their running away; what with their dread of the wild ones and their attachment to, I was going to say, their keepers, but I ought to say their rice puddings, they were sure to come in at nightfall. These rice puddings were the greatest luxury the elephant could have; a mass of boiled rice about four or five times the size of an ordinary pudding was prepared for each elephant every evening. The cook having carefully rounded the pudding would dig his fist deep down into the top of it, leaving a sort of hollow cup; this was filled with a sweet kind of oil. The elephants were then drawn up in line, and the puddings being ready, at a given signal each one threw up his trunk and opened wide his mouth, when the Mahouts popped the luscious morsel with its oily accompaniment into the mouth, and no alderman could have eaten with more gusto the green fat of the turtle than the elephants did their rice puddings.

One Sunday they did not come in for their puddings, and early on Monday morning a messenger came up quite breathless to me (my hut being about four miles from the station) to say that the tame elephants were surrounded by a herd of wild ones, that the keepers dare not go in to rescue them, begging me to come at once, as the wild ones were killing our tame ones. I lost no time in collecting my rifles and hastened down. I can hardly describe the scene I witnessed when I arrived. The forest usually so silent was now resounding in every direction with the screaming and trumpeting of the animals, and the crashing and breaking of bamboos. In fact the turmoil was quite appalling, and I had visions of my finest elephants being killed or maimed. I knew that the best thing to be done was to shoot one of the wild beasts, as that would at once disperse the herd; now as a rule, one can always distinguish the tame from the wild elephant, for the former being regularly groomed and washed is as black as a piece of India rubber, while the wild animal covers itself with mud and sand to keep off the mosquitos and flies of all kinds, so I crept up very cautiously and soon spied two very dirty-looking elephants standing under a tree. I got up to about seventeen yards of them, and taking aim at the brain of the nearest one, was actually pressing the trigger of my rifle, when I heard the clink of a chain just in time to save its life. I firmly believe that these two elephants had covered themselves with mud and sand so as not to be recognised and attacked by the wild herd around them.

There were about sixteen of the wild ones, all females with young ones, which accounted for their being so troublesome. I had great difficulty in getting up to them, and in my first attempt failed to kill one; I had to run some distance to intercept them as they were now thoroughly alarmed, and rushing through the grass which in some places was so high that I could only see the tops of their backs; suddenly an old female either saw or smelt me, and came charging through the grass right at me; to run would have been dangerous, as there were no trees to get behind, so I waited till I could see her eyes; on she came, and when she was not more than eight yards from me I let drive and planted a ball exactly between her eyes; but to my horror she did not fall; there was a stream behind me, and the hop step and a jump I made over that stream would, I think, have won me a prize at any of the athletic games of modern times. Nothing like an enraged elephant at one's back to make a long jump. As I jumped I looked over my shoulder, thinking the beast was upon me, and I saw that she had fallen dead. I immediately recrossed the stream, and with my other barrel knocked over another which was trying to pass its fallen companion; the rest of the herd rapidly dispersed, and I was glad to find that none of my tame ones had received any injury.

Elephants when in captivity are liable to become very delicate in their constitution, and are often ailing; I used to be a good deal troubled at times to know whether an elephant was ill or not, and I was obliged to depend upon the report of the head keeper as to whether the patient should have a bucket, or half a bucket of castor oil, or an opium pill strong enough to kill a dozen men. On one occasion I paid dear for interfering; a teak beam had been put down with its number underneath, and as I wanted particularly to ascertain what the number was, and there were no men available I ordered the keeper of a fine male elephant to bring him up and make him turn over the plank. The Mahout said that the elephant was not very well and could not do it; now making an elephant turn over one of these planks would be about the same as asking a railway porter to turn over a tolerable sized portmanteau; I thought the man was humbugging me, so I insisted that my order should be obeyed. When the elephant was brought up he was very reluctant to touch the plank, and it was only after some trouble we got him to turn it over; this was all he had to do; the next morning he was dead, and I made up my mind never again to attempt to force a sick elephant to do any work. These tame elephants become much attached to their keeper and his belongings; it is touching to see how gentle they are with children, I have often watched the little children of the keeper playing about between the legs of a big brute, the animal standing perfectly quiet for fear of treading upon them.

The elephant in his wild state is quite a different animal to the elephant in captivity; when roaming about the hills they are cunning and cautious to a degree, and the bulls as a rule, but not always, take the precaution to send their wives and children in advance. The old tuskers always come last in the single file in which they move when on the foray. Their olfactory organs are extremely sensitive and when

THE KNOWING OLD ENGINEER.

stalking them the direction of the wind must be most carefully considered. You may come up to within a few yards of them if care is taken in this respect. The pace they go when disturbed is marvellous, particularly when one sees the shuffling sort of movement they have. The paths they make over the ranges of hills they frequent are quite wonderful examples of engineering, and one cannot help being struck with the skill with which they are traced; the gradients are truly wonderful, avoiding every steep and difficult ascent by regular zigzags, and I could not help thinking what a knowing old engineer the first maker of the track must have been.

Wild elephants generally go in herds of from fifteen upwards; the largest herd I ever saw was on the Annamullies, it numbered at least sixty animals and was a wonderful sight. The size of the wild elephant has been often greatly exaggerated; anything over nine feet is very large, one of ten feet is a monster. Sanderson says "there is little doubt that there is not an elephant ten feet at the shoulder in India;" the account of the exciting encounter with the large tusker shot by Sir Victor Brooke, proves that at times they do exceed ten feet but it is a most rare occurrence.

Sanderson gives such an excellent and accurate description of the habits of this animal in its wild state that I need not further dwell upon the subject and will confine myself to a few examples of sport on the Neilgherries and Annamullies.

The first elephant I ever killed was on the 12th September, 1854, when at Bundipore. I started about 3.30 to the hill nearly south of the bungalow, saw a peacock airing himself and shamefully missed him. Just before this I had heard a very loud report not far off, and as I was loading, two native shikaries came up. I looked upon them with no friendly eye, but to my astonishment they told Francis, my shikarie, that there was an elephant close by at which they had fired and wounded and that it was still in the ravine; in a very short time we arrived at its edge and one of the men pointed down. It was a very deep thickly wooded place and I could see nothing; the next instant the bushes moved and I heard a kind of grunt and the great brown back of an elephant came in sight;

on creeping up I saw another, but when I was about forty yards from them they both quietly walked away; a little further on we found them standing in a small open space where a third had joined them. I crept up to some bushes and on looking through saw one of them facing me, another nearly broadside on and the third a little way behind them. Not being quite certain where to hit the one facing me, I took the one which was broadside on, aiming at the hollow over the eye, or rather between the eye and the ear; at the shot down she went, to my intense satisfaction. The others stood for an instant and then dashed away crashing through the jungle; had I been an experienced hand I might have had a crack at one of them before they bolted, but fearing that the fallen one might get up again, I reserved my shot. The two native shikaries had bolted at the very first crash. The fallen elephant, however, remained quite still, but seeing its eyes moving I went close up and put a bullet through the back of its head and afterwards a third into the hollow above the base of the trunk, but the first shot had killed her. A fine female; we cut off her tail and went our way highly delighted.

In shooting wild elephants care should always be taken that there is a tree handy to get behind in case you fail to kill and the animal charges, and every one who goes in for this sport ought to know the precise position of the brain and where to place the bullet. The diagram on the opposite page, made upon the rules drawn up by Michael, gives the various positions.

On the 6th of September, 1855, when on the Annamullies I killed my first tusker. I had breakfasted very early, and took my whole battery with me all loaded for

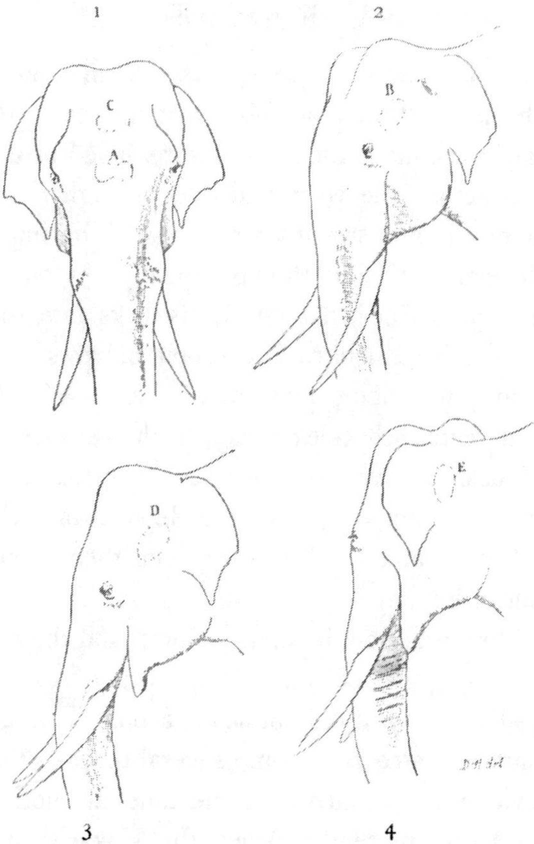

1 The A and C Shots. 2 The B Shot.
3 The D Shot. 4 The E Shot.

Explanation of diagram. The brain lies exactly between the ears —a string passed through the ears would penetrate the centre of the brain. You must always aim to cut the string in the centre. When level with you hit him in A, when ¾ towards you in B, when below you in C, when broadside on in D, right into the orifice of the ear; when ¾ away in E, you must be able to see the elephant's eye in taking this shot. If an elephant charges with trunk up you cannot kill him for certain, so get out of his way if you can. If you cannot, step on one side and let drive into his eye, it will make him wink at all events.

elephants. The head karder joined us, making five karders with me.[1] Within a short distance they struck off an elephant track made the night before, it led us up hill and down dale across the river and over a high ridge of the mountain down into swamps which would be impenetrable but for the elephant paths through them. At one place we saw where the tusker had rammed his tusks into the side of the hill. The holes looked like rabbit burrows. I put my arm to above my elbow into one of them. We afterwards got into an immensely thick swamp with reeds far above my head and bushes covered with thick creepers. I sincerely hoped we should not meet with the elephant in such a place, as if he charged and I did not drop him there would be no getting out of his way.

The scent was now becoming warm, and the excitement proportionately great, but on holding up my hand I found I was perfectly steady, it did not shake a bit. The tusker had crossed and recrossed the swamp several times—at one place he had evidently remained for some time, at another he had taken his bath; presently, Atley, the shikarie, heard him ahead, we hurried to get round him, but before we could overtake him he had passed out of the thick jungle at the head of the swamp on to some rising ground clear of the jungle; we pushed on, for there was no time to be lost as it was nearly five o'clock. Presently, Atley saw him, and in an intense state of excitement pointed to some reeds in a small swamp, and I caught sight of his great brown back above them; we crept up close till I could see his head, but he was

---

[1] The karders are the native inhabitants of these hills and are excellent trackers.

still over thirty paces from me. I wanted to get nearer but they told me to fire, so I aimed to hit him between the eye and ear. At the shot down he went, but my exultation was short-lived, for he kicked up a tremendous dust, evidently trying to get on his legs again, and before I could get down my side of the ravine he was going up the other as if nothing had happened. I fired at him again, with a projectile, aiming behind the ear; it stopped and staggered him, but he held on, going very slowly. We managed by running quickly to get in front of him; and as we came to a bit of open forest posted ourselves behind a large tree. We heard him below us crashing through a thick clump of bamboo; presently he appeared right in front of us going up the hill, head low, and looking very groggy. I advanced a pace or two from the tree, knelt down so as to get low enough for the shot between the eyes, took a steady aim and sent a projectile into his brain; he fell dead on his side without a struggle. Vyapooree, the head karder, made me fire a couple more shots to make sure, which I did, although I felt certain he was quite dead. The karders were highly delighted. I measured him round the forefoot and from the foot to the shoulder; twice the circumference of the former exactly corresponded with the latter, viz., nine feet eight inches; his tusk at the thickest part was sixteen and a half inches in circumference—one four feet nine and the other four feet eight in length. It was just five o'clock when I killed him, and we were a long way from home. We lost the path in the dark, and had to grope our way through the jungle to the river, and it was no easy work crossing; I was once or twice nearly down amongst the rocks and stones; but the kaders brought me home safely.

On Friday, November 9th, 1855, I had a most exciting adventure with a tusker. After an early breakfast, I started at six o'clock a.m. to look for elephants with my battery of four guns, and after some time we hit upon a last night's track; it got mixed up with others on the banks of a stream, and the karders did not seem to be carrying it on satisfactorily to themselves, when one of them suddenly struck upon a fresh track with the droppings not cold in the centre. We had not proceeded very far when the leading karder (a Takedy man) suddenly retreated upon me; I expected he had come on the elephant, but on stepping forward saw in a small open space a bear grubbing for food. After effectually accounting for him and another, we carried on the spoor of the elephant, and shortly came to signs that he was not far ahead; we soon heard him, and then saw his great body through the bamboos. I ran on with the big rifle and waited for him on the other side of a clump, some fifteen yards or so from me, and on his head appearing, I saw he was a tusker; I took a steady aim between the eye and ear and down he went, but from the way he fell I knew he was not killed. I ran up to him and put a couple of projectiles behind his ear as he got on his legs again, but they failed to drop him, and then after firing another apparently well-placed shot which had not the slightest effect upon him, I became so excited and so afraid of losing him, that I fired one or two shots at random, and on attempting to reload found to my intense disgust that I had no more powder. I had foolishly brought out with me my small powder horn, forgetting that the large charges for elephants would soon empty it.

I had now only one charge left. The elephant was so

badly wounded that he could not go out of a slow walk, and I saw that one eye was closed, so I ran up on his blind side and getting a little forward fired my last shot between the eye and ear; down he fell and I thought the victory was mine, but no, to my astonishment I saw him slowly rise again and walk off. From the way he ran against trees and bamboos I made certain he was quite blind; he crossed the stream again and went a short way

I try to drive him home
but only drive him furious

up the opposite side, I stole near him and then plainly saw that my surmise was correct. It was then about ten o'clock, so I determined to stand guard over him all day, and an extraordinary day's guard it was. I found he was without a tail, every particle of which had been eaten away by disease, and this tailless behind of his appeared to give him much trouble, as he several times calmly scratched it against a tree.

It was a sight to see him come against a good sized tree and knock it down, but the bamboo clumps bothered him extremely; he pushed up against them with all his force, they cracked and split and bent, but he could not force his way through them; his rage at times was very great, he would knock a tree down, trample it under foot and kick it backwards and forwards. I tried to induce him to move towards Takedy by occasionally throwing a stone at him, but this only made him still more furious, so finding we could do no more with him in the way of driving him I left him alone, and as it was near five o'clock and he was evidently getting weaker and could not go far we returned home. The next morning I went out to look for him and found him dead a few yards beyond where we had left him on the previous evening. I made him by measurement nine feet two inches at the shoulder, and his tusks one foot five and a half and one foot five in circumference, five feet four and a half inches and four feet nine inches respectively in length.

On the 20th September, 1856, I started for a day at Perevai-Colum, my principal object being to try if I could kill a buck cheetul. As the elephant keepers wanted meat I took two of them with me, but just beyond the first nullah Atley pulled up at the fresh track of a herd of elephants; I sent the Mussulmen back, and away we went after the Hutties. Early in the chase we came upon two bull bison feeding together, they were both fine, but one of them was particularly handsome with fine wide-spreading horns; what a snort he gave as he stood broadside on, wondering where the strange noise came from (I was tapping the stock of my rifle with my hand). How I should like to have plugged him, but the track of the elephants was so fresh that I was obliged to refrain; at last they quietly walked away without seeing us. We came to a long check, having got on to a last night's track, but again hitting off the right track away we went for some miles, and at last heard the loud crashing of bamboos ahead. The wind being unfavourable we circled round, and approaching very carefully soon saw a big head; and we heard other elephants beyond. Atley pointed to the head we had first seen. I whispered that I could see no tusks, but he

said "That's a big one." I crept up to a tree within ten or twelve paces of him as he stood on the other side of a very thin bamboo clump facing me. The front of his head was quite clear, so kneeling down on one knee to obtain a better angle I fired my rifle loaded with a spherical ball, and four and a half ounces of powder; to my astonishment it did not even stop him, and before I could get the other rifle he had turned and bolted. I took a crack at the side of his head as he rushed through the bamboos, and another at his ear; both shots appeared to stagger him. I kept running and watching for a favourable turn of his head, but he never stopped and made for some open forest. In passing through the bamboos he or we had disturbed a bull bison, which ran across the elephant's path, who immediately charged him furiously, and Atley declared struck him with his tusks, which so alarmed the bison that he put on his best pace and soon outran the elephant, who continued to chase him for some minutes. I tried to run on but got so blown I was obliged to give it up.

On the 11th October, 1856, Michael and I started after an early breakfast to Pullikul on the chance of falling in with elephants. Pullikul means "child's stone." The karder women who love their lords come to it, and standing on a flat stone a few yards from the Pullikul, which is a round projecting piece of rock, place a stone on their toes and attempt to pitch it on the rock; if it happens to alight on the rock, the child will be a boy, if it hits and falls back, a girl, and if they fail to strike the rock at all the child will die at its birth. We wandered through the forest till nearly one o'clock without seeing anything but some tracks of bison and the quite fresh "pug" of a tiger.

It should be mentioned that at this time (1856) the elephants were very numerous in Southern India, and had committed so many depredations in the cultivated districts that the Government had issued an order for all elephants to be killed, and offered a reward for each elephant, male or female; had this not been the case no females would have been shot. We had just sat down to tiffin when Atley pointed to the fresh track of an elephant; as soon as we had tiffed we took up the track. It was not long before we got up to the herd feeding in some open forest; I pointed out the tusker to Michael, whose turn it was, and who went down to him, I keeping more to the left where there were two or three females; on seeing him raise his rifle I cocked mine, when bang it went off. I had got into the bad habit of cocking my rifle without noise by drawing the trigger back as I pulled up the hammer—a most dangerous plan. I was most awfully disgusted at the contretemps and fully expected that Michael would lose the tusker by it. I ran back to get another rifle and returned just in time to see an old female blundering over a prostrate companion. They had given me the Laing rifle and I bowled her over with a shot behind the ear, she falling on the top of the dead one. The row was now something awful, and to my astonishment I found in this short time Michael had dropped the tusker and a brace of females. The row was caused by two little elephant calves; one had got its tail jammed between the two dead females, which made him sing out most lustily, and the other joined in the chorus; added to this, were the groans and grunts of one of the fallen elephants and the roaring of another tusker a short distance off, which Michael ran up to and shot. We then ran some distance after another tusker till we were both quite out of breath, and when we stopped, found ourselves near one of the calves. The little beast was roaring like half a dozen tigers—such a queer little brute about the size of a wild boar, and looking like an elephant dwarf at least two hundred years old. We laid ourselves out to catch him, and now commenced as laughable a scene as ever occurred. The little brute was the most perfect caricature of an enraged

THE TABLES TURNED.

WE HELD ON LIKE "GRIM DEATH."

HELP! HELP!!

WE SECURE HIM AT LAST.

tusker, charging right and left at everything that came in his way, banging his head up against enormous forest trees, and pushing with all his force against them, apparently under the impression that they must fall beneath his enormous power. On my trying to turn him he furiously charged me, turning as I turned, roaring at me with rage, and when I got behind a tree he came full tilt up against it. At last we boned him by the tail, and held on over a fallen tree like grim death; however, the strong little brute gradually worked his tail through our hands and ran off again. We tore after him and I caught him by his tail again, shouting out loudly for assistance; he dragged us to the edge of a rock and Michael neatly pushed him over it, we holding by the tail so that he could not use his hind legs; after many hard struggles and stretching his tail and trunk to the utmost we secured him, but the poor little beast died the next day.

On the 14th we were undecided where we should go, when the question was settled by Atley reporting that a tusker had been seen on the other side of the Annagundy Pass, with fresh tracks of a herd. We started about nine a.m., riding as far as the top of the Pass; we had gone but a very short distance down the other side when we struck on the "spoor" of the herd; some monkeys in the reeds close by made a sound so exactly like elephants moving off that for a time we thought that they had taken alarm, but it was not so, for after a comparatively short track we came up with them. We could only see a couple of females low down in a nullah. I selected one showing the temple shot, though it was the furthest off, as I funked the shot behind the ear which the nearest gave. This deceived Michael, who thought I was sure to take the nearest; seeing me raise my rifle, he did the same and at my report was considerably astonished to see the elephant he was aiming at fall; he consequently only got a running shot at the other, and failed to drop her. I had fired the big rifle with the conical ball, which only knocked the elephant's head into a bamboo clump on the opposite bank; after staggering about she got on her legs again and com-

HEELS OVER HEAD.

menced climbing up the bank. I now had a capital lesson on the ear shot, for Michael was at my elbow showing me the exact spot where to plant the bullet. On receiving the shot the elephant reared up on end and fell clean heels over head to the bottom of the nullah, such an awful smash—squelch would be a better term. Michael said he had never seen anything like it. She was a very large female; I made her with the measuring tape eight feet seven inches.

In 1863, when at Hassanoor with the late Sir Victor Brooke, he shot the largest elephant ever killed in Southern India. We had started early on the morning of the 30th of July, the native shikaries being very positive about elephants being in the neighbourhood. We had not gone far before fresh marks and droppings dispelled all doubts, and shortly afterwards we came plump on a tusker standing amongst some low trees. We crept up to within twelve yards of him, but just as B. fired, the elephant had raised his head and was apparently picking his teeth with his trunk; this threw the angle out and the ball went in front of the brain, or rather past it. He wheeled round at the shot, and I caught him an awful smite on the other ear with the Lancaster, which nearly brought him down, but he recovered himself and went off at a great rate. B. took up the running and was very close to him at one time, but he got away; he was not a very large animal, but his ivories were worth bagging. We returned to the bungalow to breakfast, B. a good deal cut up at the loss of the tusker. Soon after breakfast a number of elephants were reported about three miles off in the other valley through which the road passes, so away we went after them; heard them in the valley below us, and presently saw some of them on the opposite side; just then some men minding cattle hearing one of the elephants trumpeting began shouting "Anee, Anee!" (Elephants, Elephants) which put the whole herd in motion. They all passed along a rather open space of the hill about a quarter of a mile distant. I never saw such a sight—there were at least sixty elephants, the leader being a splendid old bull; on they went, sometimes in twos and threes, sometimes in single file; with two or three small tuskers, and last of all, whipping them in, came a monster; his tusks appeared to be so long that they almost touched the ground; there was an exclamation of surprise from all present. When they had passed we followed and soon came up to them standing in rather an open glade on the hill side, and there was the grand old tusker outside of all. It was my shot by *right*, but my

THE FIRST SHOT AT THE GREAT TUSKER.

sole desire was that Brooke should bag him. There were so many elephants about, and especially one old female facing us, that it was very difficult to get nearer than thirty paces to the big bull. He was standing looking away from us close to a tree, and we then saw, alas, that he had only one tusk. It was a long shot but we could not get nearer, and as he turned his head I whispered to Brooke to take him behind the ear. The shot only spun him round, and as he exposed his other ear we both let drive, which staggered him tremendously, and with ears cocked forward he reeled about like a drunken man; I then ran forward to about twelve yards and planted a ball exactly between the eyes. Brooke followed it up with a couple from his Westley Richard rifle. I thought he must fall, but I believe he was saved by resting on his tusk for a moment; he then recovered himself and bolted. He dashed down into a deep ravine and gave a loud roar; on running up

THE DEATH OF THE GREAT TUSKER OF HASSANOOR.

he was nowhere to be seen, so we took up the track, at first there was no difficulty, but this, from the blood ceasing, increased; still, on we went, Brooke manfully sticking to the track, I despairing of ever seeing the grand beast again.

For a good nine miles we followed the track, the greater part of the way at a foot trot; at last we came to the foot of a hill down which the elephant had zigzagged *at a walk.* On rounding some thick bushes the man in front of me pointed, and there was the huge monster standing in some water. Pushing Brooke to the front he steadily raised his rifle, and aiming at the orifice of the ear let drive, and down came the grand old tusker with a crash, sending up the water far above our heads. It was a long shot—twenty-seven yards. I ran down to the elephant, and seeing he was not dead Brooke killed him by a shot in the back of his head, and thus died the largest and toughest old tusker I ever came across; a grand trophy. His tusk measured five feet eleven inches outside the lip, and carefully measuring him we made him exactly eleven feet high with an enormously thick neck; although he showed no signs of great age except in his feet, he must have been, I think, a very old animal. We had seven miles to get home, but right cheerfully we accomplished the journey, Brooke doing the greater part of it with only one shoe. We did not arrive at the bungalow till long after dark.

We devoted the greater part of the next day to cutting out the tusks, and a long business it was. The broken tusk was in a very decayed state, and the fœtid odour from it almost unbearable. How the poor brute must have suffered!

In respect to the tusks of this elephant the following letter in the *Field* newspaper, from the late Sir Victor Brooke, settles the question as to their size and weight:—

"SIR—Will you kindly allow me to correct a mistake in your correspondent 'Smoothbore's' letter, published under the above heading in your issue of the 1st inst. In his letter 'Smoothbore' states that the weight of the large tusk of the elephant shot by me in the Hassanoor Hills, Southern

India, was eighty-five pounds, and that so long ago as 1870 I confirmed this statement in *The Field.* If I did so, I was myself in error. When my friend, Mr. Sanderson, published his most interesting work entitled 'Thirteen Years amongst the Wild Beasts in India,' he requested me to have the tusks of the elephant weighed and measured carefully, and at page 63 all the dimensions will be found accurately recorded. It will be seen that the perfect tusk weighs ninety pounds, and the broken one forty-nine pounds. The perfect tusk is exactly eight feet in length. Unluckily I cannot remember exactly what the tusks weighed shortly after the animal was killed, but I remember being disappointed at finding they had lost considerably when I weighed them for Mr. Sanderson, *i.e.*, fourteen years afterwards.

"VICTOR BROOKE."

On this same trip I killed my last elephant. On August 1st, we started up the valley to look for elephants. When three parts up we saw some on the opposite side; it took us some time to get round, and when we did get to the spot they had vanished. After hunting about amidst numerous tracks we at last heard them; creeping up to a tree about thirty yards from them, I saw they were all females. I would not fire for fear of disturbing a tusker, so we watched them for some time, and the way in which they flogged the flies off with twigs was a caution to small boys; at last one of them winded us and they all moved off. Soon afterwards we came on them again, hidden away in some bamboos; we got up close to three females. I moved a little forwards to get the shot; the instant I did so an old lady with a calf at her heels caught sight of me and wheeled round. I had my rifle loaded with a quicksilver hardened ball and four drachms of powder. She was not above fourteen yards off. The ball struck her between the eyes, but the only effect was to turn her round and send her off at the double. I was considerably riled after such a failure, and was sitting on a rock chewing the cud of disgust when our people said there was an elephant close by. Asking B. to stop her if I did not, we stole up to her. I saw that she was the same old female with the young one; I got up to within sixteen yards, and the next moment would have had a good ear shot, but she saw me and instantly gave a trumpet and charged full tilt at us down the slope of the hill. I had to advance a pace or so to get clear of some bushes; taking a steady aim with the Lancaster I sent both balls between her eyes, and though tin hardened bullets they had apparently no more effect than if they had been putty. The Lascar with my other gun had bolted, so there was no help for it but to bolt after him; he fell flat on his face, and I got the rifle from him. In the meantime Brooke had stood like a trump, and had stopped and turned the elephant at seven or eight yards; he wisely did not wait on such ground to fire the other barrel. He said the calf, on its mother turning, threw up its trunk and gave a loud hooray, when away they both went, and we never saw them again. This was very unsatisfactory. We had not, however, gone far when we came upon a fresh herd returning up the hill from their bath; they were all covered with black mud, but there was no tusker with them; we stalked to within twenty yards of them; my two failures had nearly destroyed my confidence. After watching them for some time I took a shot at an old female behind the ear as she turned; it appeared to be another failure, but the next moment she toppled over, falling dead against a tree. She was an extraordinary old elephant; her stumps were worn down to the roots, she had not a particle of hair on her tail, and her general appearance shewed signs of great age. The Lascar stood very steady this time, I had pointed out to him the danger to both of us if he ran before handing me the rifle.

"*BAFFLED.*" *(Vide Chap. VIII.)*

CHAPTER VIII.

TIGERS, LEOPARDS, &c.

TIGERS—DIFFICULTY OF SEEING THEM—AMALGAMATION OF COLOUR WITH SURROUNDING OBJECTS—TIGER WITH JACKAL—TIGERS AND WILD DOGS—THEIR FEAR OF DOGS—POWER OF TIGER'S JAWS AND LIMBS—THEIR NOISELESS MOVEMENTS—MAN EATERS—TIGER'S DREAD OF MAN—THE MODE OF STRIKING ITS PREY — RAPIDITY OF STROKE — SHOOTING TIGERS ON FOOT — DANGERS OF THE SPORT—SIR JAMES OUTRAM—HIS WONDERFUL ESCAPE—TIGERS AND SAMBUR—TIGERS AND PUTRID FLESH—POWER OF SCENT—SIR SAMUEL BAKER'S OPINION—H.R.H. DISCOVERS HIS MISTAKE—THE CHEEKY RASCAL—SIZE OF TIGERS—MY FIRST TIGER—EXCITING CHASE AFTER A TIGER —THE VULTURES WILL BRING HIM OUT—RATHER A SURPRISE—EXCITING RENCONTRE WITH THREE TIGERS—TIGER AND WILD BOAR—A FIERCE FIGHT —TIGER STARED OUT OF COUNTENANCE—LOOK OUT! HE'S COMING—WHAT I SAW ON JAN. 31, 1868—TIGER AND HINDS—MY LAST TIGER—TIGER STORIES —SHOOTING TIGERS FROM AN ELEPHANT—COLONEL GEOFFREY NIGHTINGALE'S LETTER—THE LEOPARD—THE BLACK LEOPARD—HIS DEATH—THE JUNGLE CAT—LOSS OF MY DOG SNOB—THE HARES ARE WITCHES—CLARK'S THEORY—LEOPARDS ON THE TREES—MY LAST LEOPARD.

WHILST residing on the Nielgherries, the Pulnies, and the Annamullies, I had many opportunities of observing the habits of some of the larger animals, which are very little known either to the sportsman or to the naturalist. As regards tigers, I have come across them both when after their prey or when resting in their lairs, and have watched them for an hour or two at a time when, owing to some cause, I have been unable to stalk or get near them. I always carried a very powerful telescope with which I could see almost every hair on their bodies and every expression in their faces. I have in this way interviewed over fifty tigers. It is extraordinary how difficult it is to distinguish a tiger either in the open or in the jungle; on looking at the skin with its large black stripes on a yellowish red body, with the pure white on the face, breast, and flanks, one would imagine there would be no difficulty in seeing it anywhere, but it is not so. The tawny colour so corresponds or rather amalgamates with the dry grass and leaves, and the stripes with the black shadows of the trees and bushes, that the animal becomes almost invisible. I once wounded a tiger that did not fall dead on the spot, and contrary to my usual custom I followed him, a most dangerous proceeding when shooting a tiger on foot. I had two keen-sighted natives with me. Presently we came to a spot where the jungle was rather open, with a few small trees and bushes scattered about, and dry grass a few inches high; the sun was shining brightly, casting the black shadows of the trees across the withered grass, and we stood at the edge of this open space for some minutes, straining our eyes to ascertain where the tiger had gone, suddenly one of the men said, "he dead," and there not more than ten or twelve yards from us lay the tiger stretched on the grass, stone dead, but his black stripes and yellow body so exactly corresponded with the black shadows and yellow grass, that none of us could at first make him out. Even in the open, at a few hundred yards distant, not a stripe can be distinguished on a tiger's body, and I have more than once mistaken one for a deer.

The tiger when out prowling for food is often accompanied by a single jackal, and when this is the case the jackal has a most peculiar cry or rather howl, and whenever that cry is heard you may be sure a tiger is with him. I only once saw a tiger and a jackal together; I had heard of a tiger having killed a buffalo, and went to try and get a shot at him. As I came to the place I saw him stealing away, out of rifle range, in company with the jackal which kept at a respectful distance on his flank and trotted along with his back arched showing every appearance of cringing fear. I fancy the tiger has no love for his companion and would eat him as soon as look at him if he could only get the chance.

It has been said that wild dogs will attack and kill a tiger; I doubt it; but I know that they will beset a tiger as if they were aware of his instinctive fear of the canine race. A friend of mine, a coffee planter, going round his plantation heard a curious noise in the forest bordering his estate, he cautiously stole in to see what was the matter; on going round the corner of a thick bush he almost trod upon the tail of a tiger standing with his back towards him; he silently retreated, but as he did so he saw there was a pack of wild dogs a few paces in front of the tiger yelping at him and making the peculiar noise which had previously attracted his attention. Having procured his rifle he returned with some of his men to the spot; the tiger was gone but they disturbed a large pack of wild dogs feeding on the body of a stag, which on examination was found to have been killed by the tiger for there were marks of its teeth in the stag's neck. The dogs had evidently driven him from his prey.

The inhabitants of the Nielgherry hills only discovered the tiger's dread of dogs a short time before I left India. These hills are undulating and interspersed with detached woods (sholas) and forests; occasionally in one of these sholas a tiger will take up his quarters, and when this is discovered a party would be formed to slay him. The plan latterly adopted was to collect a pack of all kinds of dogs, and put them on the track of the tiger; they invariably either drove him out of the wood, or up a tree; and somehow or other they generally managed to kill him. It is worthy of notice that a tiger will hardly ever get up a tree unless thus scared by dogs.

I know nothing more convincing of the extraordinary strength of a tiger both in the power of jaw and muscle than to see what he does with a large dead buffalo or an old bull bison. Now an old bull bison stands six feet at the shoulder, and is about nine feet long from his chest to his hind quarters, and is of great bulk, certainly half as large again as an ordinary bull. I have known the body of this huge beast turned completely round by a tiger, and I have seen large buffaloes which have been picketed, killed by a tiger and dragged into the jungle to a considerable distance.

I have at times been astonished at the perfectly noiseless movements of this animal; on one occasion I was watching the carcass of a buffalo that had been killed by a tiger, he had dragged it into a thicket and I was sitting on the branch of a tree waiting for him. It was a perfectly still calm day and no rain having fallen for some time, the jungle was quite dried up, and the dead leaves strewn about made such a noise when trodden on that I fancied a mouse could not pass over them without my hearing it. I had been watching for some time, when I heard what I fancied was a stick fall on the dry leaves, this put me on the alert and I listened with strained ears but there was not another sound; I had just leaned back again, thinking it was nothing, when the tiger suddenly appeared like a ghost not twenty paces from me. One can fancy what an advantage this noiseless movement is to the tiger in procuring his prey, and what a terribly dangerous brute he becomes when he makes use of it in stealing on some unfortunate human being. This brings me to say a few words about the man-eaters. Man-eating tigers are usually supposed to be old mangy brutes that have lost their teeth and power, and take to killing human beings as the easiest means of procuring food, but it is often the case that man-eaters are fine healthy young tigers with all their teeth perfect and in good condition. Now supposing a man-eater to be a tigress who has discovered how easy it is to take a man at work in the woods, or a woman stooping to get water at a nullah; her cubs having for some time been living on human flesh, and having seen their mother kill her victims in this way, would become man-eaters themselves. There was a famous man-eating tigress at the foot of the Nielgherry hills when I was there, which was known to have killed more than two hundred human beings and a large reward was offered for her destruction, but she was so cunning that she baffled all attempts. The jungle was often driven, but no tiger was seen; cattle were picketed, but no tigress would come near them. At last, a friend of mine happened to be on the spot when this brute had just carried off an unfortunate woman as she was getting water from a stream, he immediately collected a few men and took up the track knowing the beast would steal away directly she heard beaters. He started off and making a circuit got some distance ahead; presently he had the satisfaction of seeing the tigress crossing a dry water course not far from him; she stood for a moment to listen; that moment was her last, a well-directed shot behind the shoulder rolled her over dead. I saw the skin, it was one of the most beautiful I had ever seen, without a spot or blemish.

As a rule the man eater is more cowardly than the ordinary tiger. It prowls about villages and pounces upon some unfortunate woman or woodcutter; indeed, I have been told, but I cannot vouch for the truth, that the noise of the woodcutter's axe will attract a man-eating tiger. I have on several occasions been in the neighbourhood of man-eaters; I never liked it, but felt comparatively safe as I have never known or heard of an instance of any European or native armed and on the alert being attacked.

Most tigers are great cowards. They are nothing more than gigantic cats and we all know that cats are not very courageous animals; some cats show more courage than others, so it is with tigers, but they are quite as much afraid of meeting man, as man is of meeting them. A man knows that the tiger could kill him as easily as a cat could kill a mouse, but fortunately most tigers do not know this and have an instinctive dread of man. For the three years I was in charge of the Annamullay Teak forests, I may say I lived with tigers. I could hardly go out a day without finding fresh foot marks, yet I knew I was comparatively safe, for the karders, a race of hill men, inhabiting the forest, never hesitated to return to their homes on the darkest night, and in no instance had any of them ever been attacked by a tiger. I had, therefore, no fear of returning home through the forest after dark.

On one occasion, however, rather a creepy feeling came over me. I was forcing my way through some high grass late one evening when on looking down I saw a tiger's foot print in front of me perfectly dry, so I knew the animal was just before me; it was impossible to see more than a yard or two in this dense high grass, and my great fear was that the tiger might mistake my brown shooting dress for the body of a deer and strike me down by mistake, and it would be little use begging my pardon afterwards, so I commenced singing, as I knew that the striped gentleman or lady hates nothing so much as a human voice at a high pitch.

The tiger in the plains is seldom seen till eventide, as he generally lies up during the day in dense jungle or tangled brushwood, but in the cooler climate of the mountains he wanders about freely in the day time. I have never seen a tiger strike down an animal although I have watched him or her for an hour together prowling about on the opposite hill in search of prey. I have seen them chase deer, but they never go more than two or three hundred yards, and the magnificent bounds they take are quite thrilling to behold. Some have stated that the tiger differs in his attack from the lion, in not killing his prey by a blow from his paw; this is quite different to my experience. I once saw two large Indian buffaloes lying dead within a few feet of each other, and the herdsman told me that a tiger had suddenly bounded into the midst of a herd, had struck first one and then the other buffalo, but on his yelling and shouting had disappeared as rapidly as he had come; I examined these dead beasts and found that both of them had their necks broken. A friend of mine told me that he was once out after a tiger that had laid up in a sugar cane field. Elephants and beaters were sent in to drive him out; my friend was posted on an elephant commanding the corner of the field; a native was stationed some distance further down; presently there was a shout from the beaters, and the tiger came bounding out exactly where the native was posted; on seeing him the tiger sprang clean over his head, and my friend said he could just perceive a slight motion of the tiger's forepaws as he passed over the man's head; the native fell to the ground, and on going up to him they found him lying dead with his neck broken.

I have pursued and shot all my tigers either on foot or from a ladder (never from an elephant) and with one exception have never been in danger. I have always managed to have my sport without any injury to myself or my shikaries by taking the following precautions; never firing at a tiger when facing me, never following a wounded tiger into thick jungle, and never going up to one supposed to be dead without first ascertaining beyond doubt that such is the case, or by giving the *coup-de-grace* in the shape of a ball behind the ear.

By not being careful in this respect one of our greatest Indian warriors, Sir James Outram nearly lost his life. He told me the following adventure and narrow escape he had from a tiger.

He was out on foot and had wounded a tiger which got into some low bush jungle and could not be found; he and a friend who was with him separated to look for it, for a long time without success; at last Outram came to a very dense bush, he stooped down to peer into it and had no sooner done so than the tiger sprang out at him. The charge was so rapid that he had no time to bring the rifle to his shoulder and so fired from his hip. The next moment the tiger knocked him down and was on the top of him. Outram said he felt at once that the tiger was dead, but the great weight of the animal prevented him freeing himself;

his friend hearing the shot came running up and seeing the tiger lying on Outram was about to fire when Outram called out "don't fire, he's dead, come and pull him off me," and strange to say he escaped without a scratch. The bullet fortunately had struck the tiger at the junction of the head and neck, severing the spine, killing it instantaneously.

Two tigers will often hunt in concert, generally in couples. I have often watched them acting thus when ap-

TIGERS AND SAMBUR.

proaching a herd of deer. A brother officer told me that he saw a tiger drive a deer up to some rocks where another one was crouching ready to spring upon it. On one occasion whilst out looking for sambur, I saw a stag out feeding above a strip of jungle and noticed a tiger stealing along below it. The deer began bellowing and moved up the hill followed by the tiger, the latter trotting after the deer and occasionally breaking into a canter, the deer trotting on with its tail up. The tiger did not attempt to stalk except by remaining for a moment at a rock. The stag broke into a gallop and the tiger immediately followed it, just then my shikarie said, "look, there's another tiger above," and there was one bounding down the hill to cut off the deer, they all three disappeared in a dip, and shortly afterwards we saw the stag making away at a good pace; I watched some time hoping the tigers would re-appear, but I never saw them again. There were other sambur on the slopes and all of them were evidently aware of tigers being about.

I have occasionally come across a whole family of tigers; I once saw five pass before me a very short distance off, they were evidently migrating, and I have the idea that the old tigers were taking their now nearly full grown cubs who were quite capable of providing for themselves, to a new hunting ground, with a gentle hint not to come back to their parents. I believe the young remain with or near the old ones for some time after they are able to procure their own food; those I have seen with the parents were all nearly full grown.

Much difference of opinion has prevailed as to tigers eating animals not killed by themselves and as to their peculiar preference to putrid flesh. The following extracts from a letter on this subject in the *Oriental Sporting Magazine* of 1874, fully corroborate my own experience:—

" *Hawkeye* whose experience as a *shikarie* in this country amounts to little short of half a century, and who may safely be reckoned a thoroughly competent authority in all that pertains to *shikar*, writes thus:—

"'That tigers will eat what they do not kill I have had early 'experience:—We left a stag which was shot late in the after- 'noon, and on going to cut it up the following morning, we 'found a tiger had dragged the carcass into a *shola* not very far 'off, where the antlers of the stag got locked between the stems 'of two trees, and the tiger was obliged to make his meal 'there, which he did to the extent of the greater portion of 'the haunches.'"

"And in a letter contributed to the *South of India Observer* of November 26th, 1869, he says:—

"'Tigers are not particular as to the state of their food being 'fresh or otherwise. It was observed in the —— that these 'animals seldom—indeed never—were found to resort to the 'carcasses of the bisons that had been shot until the effluvia from 'them was exceedingly strong, indeed, it may be said when in 'the highest state of putrefaction; and, on one occasion, when 'the tiger had dragged the putrefied carcass some distance, the 'sportsman was able to follow it up to the spot by the scent, and 'found the tiger quietly reposing close to the offensive remnants 'of the bison. But we know that whenever a tiger kills game or 'cattle, if undisturbed, he returns to his prey until (with or with- 'out the help of jackals or vultures), the whole is consumed, and 'it must then be pretty high; In many cases it has been noticed 'that he makes his lair conveniently near at hand to protect the 'intrusion of any such assistants in the demolition of the carcass. 'On one occasion I was present when the noise of the descent of 'a large number of vultures on a dead buffalo lying just outside 'a *shola*, caused the tiger, who had killed it, to put in an 'appearance at noon day and protest his rights to the beef from 'the feathered tribe, and not one of the birds would go near the 'body so long as Mr. Stripes was in sight.'"

"Colonel Douglas Hamilton, in his journal, thus graphically describes an incident to the same effect:—

"'Yesterday, the last day of the month, I went out about 'mid-day (it was a wet morning) with the avaricious hope of 'adding something more to the month's bag. My first point 'was to visit the carcass of the bison I killed last Monday, '*i.e.*, yesterday week, and if a tiger was there to bag him 'first, and then go on and bag something else. I expressed 'myself to this effect to my friend before starting. Well, 'when I arrived at the spot where I left the dead bison, lo 'and behold it was not there! A broad trail, showed pretty 'plainly that a tiger had carried it off to a more convenient 'dining-room. We crept along as lightly as mice after the 'missing carcass. By Jove, we might have shut our eyes and 'hunted it, the drag stunk so! About two hundred yards 'down the hill we came on the remains of His Royal 'Highness's first meal, which appears to have consisted of 'about half the bison. As I was peering round I beheld, at the 'foot of a rock, a good deal concealed by bamboos and bushes, 'the long striped hide of the tiger himself lying at full length on 'his side. * * * I was, I should say, between forty and fifty 'paces off, and at first could not tell where his head was, whether 'towards or away from me; but his suddenly putting his paw over 'his head to brush away flies gave me the required information. 'Cocking my rifle I took a deliberate pot to catch him in the 'chest, just under the armpit. No savage roar replied to the re-'port, but the tiger sprung to his feet, and I sprung out of sight.'"

"During my experience of over a score of years as a *shikarie* in the Soonderbuns, the haunt *par excellence* of the royal quarry, I have frequently found tigers feeding on game shot by me, and that they prefer to wait to eat it until such time as it sends forth a highly unpleasant odour. Out of the many instances that I remember I shall select one which I think rather curious, and calculated to interest the reader.

"Many years ago, as I was sailing down the Passur river

in the Soonderbuns, I observed a rather large sized crocodile (our so-called alligator), and having succeeded in getting within a couple of hundred yards or so of him, I managed to place a ball from my rifle into his neck, which turned him over; another leaden bolus lodged exactly behind his shoulder, gave him his *coup de grace*, and enabled me effectually to secure him. As I was journeying to a location, which was not far from there, and as the skull and skin of 'the monster of the deep' was well worth preserving, being about seventeen feet in length, I attached a stout coir rope round its neck, and towed it on. I arrived at my destination rather late in the afternoon, and hauled the carcass on shore, leaving it about twenty to thirty paces from the *ghat* or landing place, off which the *bholio* or accommodation boat was anchored, to be there operated on the following day.

"The next morning I was rather surprised to learn that the *corpus* was *non est inventus*, and on going to the spot to investigate into the cause of its sudden disappearance, I at once discovered that it had been carried, or rather dragged away by a tiger, as the animal had left impressions of his immense feet clearly discernible on the soft ground round about. I followed the trail into some *null*, a species of red jungle, not far from the place where my boat was put up, and soon came upon the carcass, which I found untasted by the tiger. I left it where I found it in hopes of getting a shot at the audacious robber, should he return to appropriate the spoil, but it remained untouched for three successive days, when I thought it useless to keep watch over it any longer; and the stink from it was awfully bad, as decomposition had then set in. The next morning, on going to secure the skull, I was a good deal astonished to find it gone! The tiger had evidently returned at night, and after demolishing a large portion of the rotten carcass, had coolly walked off with my prize, *i.e.*, the *caput*. To be baulked in this impudent manner riled me not a little, and I searched far and wide for either my stolen property, or the bold thief, or both, but I was altogether unsuccessful. However, Mr. Tiger taught me a lesson then which has stood me in good stead ever afterwards, as I could never forget the cool way in which I had been so cleverly done.

"The plan usually adopted by the tiger is to allow the game he has killed, or others have killed to remain till the flesh stinks and becomes soft, when he sets to and devours all he can, in fact gormandizes himself to a fearful extent, so much so, that he becomes slothful for a time and remains generally close to the spot. But the tiger, while his food is commencing to undergo the process of decomposition, in order to suit his vitiated palate, is careful to remain in close proximity to it, lest some intruder should make away with the carrion. I, on several occasions, have seen the bodies of wood-cutters, who have been taken away by tigers, rescued several days after, close to the lairs of the man-eaters, almost untouched. I once most unexpectedly disturbed a brace of tigers, apparently male and female, in fine, husband and wife, feasting on the putrid remains of a rhinocerous killed a week before. *Par parenthese*, one of above tigers was shot the next day while feeding on the perfectly rotten remnants of the rhino."

"The above array of facts ought to convince all, aye, even the most sceptical, that tigers will eat game killed by the shikarie, and that they relish it when it is putrescent."

"Apart from the interest naturally felt by all of us in common in acquiring accurate information regarding the feeding habits of the royal quarry, the result of this enquiry will supply the sportsman with such knowledge as cannot but prove of immense practical value to him; if the tiger in reality evinces a *penchant* for eating game killed by others when it becomes putrid, the sportsman in future, instead of offering him a living bait in the shape of a fat ox tethered close to his haunts, to induce him to show himself, will use a more tempting bait, to wit, a stinking carcass, the scent of which he can sniff from afar. Moreover, the former plan, which is now adopted, has a smack of cruelty which cannot but be distasteful to the true sportsman, and he would gladly avoid it."

"P.S.—I have just found that our accomplished Indian naturalist who, alas! has recently been numbered with the dead—I mean the late Mr. Blyth—was well aware that tigers will eat animals killed by others, *vide Indian Sporting Review*, New Series, No. 1. In the third number of the same periodical, *Hogspear* (Mr. F. Bruce Simson, B.C.S., who is reputed on good authority to have shot during his brilliant career as a sportsman in this country literally hundreds of tigers), also expresses the same opinion. He says, 'many persons think tigers only eat the flesh of animals which they kill.' *Hogspear* then goes on to relate a lengthy tale—too lengthy to be tacked on to the fag-end of this article, or I would gladly give it,—which shows that tigers will feed on the carcass of even one of their own kind; this was established beyond doubt by the discovery of large pieces of striped skins inside the stomachs of a tigress and her cub, which had been shot near the spot where the body of a tiger (killed by a native *shikarie* the previous day with a poisoned arrow) was found partially devoured. They must have been ravenously hungry, indeed."

In a second postscript he says: "I have only this moment returned from viewing the carcass of a cow killed by a tiger yesterday. I shall very briefly describe what I witnessed while I retain a vivid recollection of the facts. The tiger had killed the bullock in the open, about a couple of hundred yards from a long stretch of very dense jungle into which he had dragged it. No one had been to the spot before I went there this afternoon, so the tiger must be allowed to have had every opportunity of having a tug into fresh beef, if so disposed, undisturbed, notwithstanding which the carcass remains entire, with the exception of a very small piece. The tiger must be somewhere in the jungle, not far from his food, for I observed a flock of vultures (*Gyps bengalensis*) on the *qui vive*, but at a respectful distance from the carcass. Press of business elsewhere, which cannot be postponed, compels me most reluctantly to quit this place, Kainmaree, this evening, or I should, I daresay, have been able to give a good account of the marauder. *Shikaries* and *ryots* hereabouts in the Soonderbuns tell me, that unless the tiger is very hungry indeed, or is in dread of being disturbed, he will not feed on his kill till putrefaction fairly sets in.

"*Apropos* of the superior felines eating game killed by the sportsman, I cannot resist the temptation of quoting a sentence from Gordon Cumming's 'Lion Hunting in South Africa,' which I chanced to see on opening his book just now:—'Lions do not refuse, as has been asserted, to feast upon the venison they have not killed themselves.' Examples of their having done so are then related.

"'I have only just received a letter from *Hawkeye*, and cannot refrain from quoting a passage from a letter he received from General B. having reference to the points herein discussed at some length. It runs as follows:—

"'TIGERS EATING PUTRID FLESH.

"'My experience goes to prove they prefer putrid to fresh 'animals, though they drink of the blood, and unless disturbed, 'take a whet off the flanks or udder, just when they have 'killed, but, in regard to their returning to dinner, there is 'nothing certain whereon to go, for I have known them 'not to return the same night, but to do so the night after, 'when putrefaction has well set in; then, again, I have 'known them to return the same afternoon, *ergo*, there is no 'certainty—no more than what a tusker you are following 'will do. On this *Hawkeye* remarks, the latter portion qualifies 'his first assertion, but there is to my mind no doubt as to 'the fact that they eat putrid flesh, but whether they actually 'prefer it we cannot pronounce until we are acquainted with 'feline language.'"

"I think I have already satisfactorily shown the reason of tigers *occasionally* eating fresh meat; I have accounted for their so doing by pointing out that they only so do when pressed by hunger, or when apprehensive of being disturbed."

Tigers are very fond of the flesh of porcupines; I have on several occasions come on places where one of these animals has been killed by a tiger. I fancy that he must lie in wait for his prey as the only vulnerable part of a porcupine is his head. It seems from the way that the quills are dispersed that he takes them out with his mouth, much as a hawk picks a bird of his feathers; sometimes in his eagerness to make his feast he tries to swallow the skin with the undergrowth of young quills, and I know of one instance where a fine tiger was choked to death by them.

It has been stated that tigers hunt their prey by scent as dogs hunt a hare or fox, and that they can wind you as deer do. I have taken particular pains to ascertain whether this is the fact, and I am almost, I may say quite, sure that it is not; although like all other animals they have large olfactory nerves they have not that peculiar sensitiveness of the organs of smell which prevails in the Canidæ or Cervidæ. I have watched tigers over and over again when out after prey, and I never saw them put their nose to the ground or hunt by scent; moreover they have no idea of taking advantage of the wind when stalking. I have seen two tigers watching a stag, like two cats watching a mousehole, with the wind blowing straight from them to the deer, which naturally soon made itself scarce. I maintain that if tigers added the power of hunting by scent, and stalking up wind, to their wonderful sight and keen sense of hearing, to say nothing of the absolute noiselessness of their movements, they would seldom or never fail in securing their prey, and this would be against the law of nature, which always allows a certain number of chances to the weaker animals, otherwise they would be exterminated.

I may here mention the curious behaviour of a tiger, which I have noticed more than once. Many of the woods on the Nielgherry plateau are isolated, and dotted about the open grassy hills and slopes, varying in size from a mere patch to several acres. On one occasion I was out looking for deer with a friend when we heard a sambur bell in one of these woods; presently another sambur joined in. I whispered to my companion that I thought there must be a tiger in the wood. I had hardly spoken when we heard a low gutteral growl; and every time the deer belled the tiger answered with a growl. Then a third deer commenced belling, and for several minutes this went on, the tiger answering with a growl, every bell of the deer. We were standing outside the wood, and from the sound, the tiger appeared to be approaching towards us, when suddenly the growling ceased, but the belling of the deer continued. A short time afterwards a hind came dashing out into the open, but no tiger appeared. I have heard a tiger growl to the bell of a sambur at other times, but never so persistently as on this occasion. Now, my idea is that the tiger by growling sets all the deer belling, and when he has fixed on the exact spot where one may be standing he suddenly stops answering, and proceeds to stalk the animal. I have little doubt that the hind which came rushing out to us had been stalked by the tiger. If the tiger had sufficient sense of smell to hunt the deer by scent, I do not think he would reply to their cry of alarm with a growl.

Sir Samuel Baker states that the tiger differs from the cat in its peculiar fondness for water. We all know that a tiger will seldom take his meal except when he is near water and will even drag a buffalo or goat a long distance so that he should be able to slake his thirst after he has fed, and will even enter a stream and lie down in it so as to be able to lap without any trouble. Tigers have been known to swim large rivers, and even an arm of the sea, but that has been done from necessity in order to obtain their food; but that it is partial to water in any other way I cannot believe, as I have never seen a tiger frequent the numerous wallowing pools in the Nielgherries or Annamullies, or a sign of one ever having used them.

Tigers when near habitations become sometimes a little too familiar, and in the shade of the evening may mistake yourself or your pony for a sambur. One evening on returning home rather late I was aware of something creeping along parallel with me, and getting nearer, I suddenly saw it was a tiger, and at the same moment H.R.H. discovered his mistake and with a smothered growl sprung away into the jungle.

Another day when I had been out after deer it came on foggy, I lost my way, and when I got back to the rocks where I had told my man to stop, he was no where to be seen; at last I spied him at the top of a hill, and called him to come down, but it was some time before he did so. I saw he looked scared, and he then told me that he had returned to the rocks, and while sitting there, he saw far up the hill what he thought was me beckoning him to come up, so up he went. Imagine his astonishment when on getting near, instead of me, he saw a tiger lying down switching its tail. I doubted the story, but swearing it was true he took me up and pointed to the unmistakeable fresh foot prints of a tiger where he had bounded down the hill into the shola below. I could not find the horse boy with the pony, who I had also told to meet me at the top of the hill, and being afraid he would get lost, I fired several shots without any effect, so went home. I found him at the hut in a great state of mind; he told me he was standing waiting for me when the pony suddenly gave a plunge and broke away from him, and on looking round for the cause, to his horror he saw a tiger stealing towards them. As may be supposed, the lad did not remain long without bolting; the pony came home in one direction and he in another.

I suppose this is what it will come to next.' the cheeky rascal.

In respect to the size of tigers, the old Forest Ranger gives the length of a full-grown tiger from point of nose to point of tail as 9 feet 5 inches.

	F.	I.
Length of tail	2	10
Height from heel to shoulder	3	2
Girth of body behind shoulder ...	5	3
Girth of forearm	2	7
Girth of neck	3	0
Circumference of head	3	3

Jerdon gives the average length of a full-grown male tiger from 9 feet to 9 feet 6 inches. Occasionally one is killed 10 feet.

	F.	I.
Shakespeare records one of ...	10	8
Simpson records two of	10	4
With height of shoulder	4	0
Nightingale records one	10	2
With height of shoulder ...	4	2

	F.	I.
The largest I have killed was ...	9	3
Height at shoulder	3	6

I killed my first tiger when out at the Avalanche on August 9, 1854. After having shot a splendid old saddle back with grand horns, I was descending the mountain towards the bungalow; about half way down I saw something outside the shola, at first I thought it was a couple of jungle sheep lying down, but on another look I saw stripes, and on bringing the glasses to bear I saw it was a royal tiger stretched out at full length on the grass. I told Francis what it was, and he said we must kill him. The ground was favourable for the stalk as the animal was lying in a little dip; we crept cautiously up to the mound above the tiger, and on looking over I saw his immense head and neck; at first I thought he was looking at me, but it was just the contrary, he was looking straight before him. At that moment a couple of shots were fired near the bungalow and the tiger turned his head in that direction, giving me a beautiful shot behind the ear; I took a steady aim and pulled; he fell over with a smothered roar. I retreated under cover of the hill, but felt certain he was dead, and sure enough when we got a sight of him again, there he was lying exactly in the same place. I returned to the mound where I first fired at him and Francis begged I would put another bullet into him, so I fired at his chest and he drew all his legs together and curled his tail over his back and thus remained. I rather wanted to go up to him, but Francis said, "if he is dead he will be there to-morrow, and if he is not he is best left alone," and so after another good look we left him for the night, and I arrived at the bungalow just at dark uncommonly proud of my afternoon's shikar—went to bed, and dreamt of tigers which were killed over night and not to be found again. After breakfast the next morning we went off, and my mind was put at rest when I saw the grand beast lying in the same spot I had left him on the preceding evening; he certainly was a splendid fellow, a four year old male in splendid condition, with a beautiful skin.

On another occasion when at the hut, I went to the ibex ground to look for sambur, and as I was going down the long hill I saw something crossing the nullah at the bottom; it looked like a large light-coloured stag, but on putting up the glasses I saw it was a tiger. He appeared to catch sight of us and slowly walked towards the shola on my right, but after approaching close to its edge, turned back again and rubbed his face against the leaves of a bush, then laid down on the bank; being on the open hill side there was no way of getting down to him without being seen. He soon sat up again, crossed the stream towards another shola, but after a few paces again lay down and began rolling about on his back. Whilst thus occupied I took the opportunity of crossing the hill and getting under the lee of the shola he was making for, and when under cover I stopped and put some fresh powder on the nipples of my rifle, and whilst doing so missed a fine opportunity, for the tiger had passed along the other side of the stream. I ran up as hard as I could, a tree between us preventing his seeing me, but when I got to the tree he was too far off. I ran down and up a dip beyond; the brute was walking steadily on straight away from me, and as there appeared no chance of getting up to him and not liking to run close to him on level ground, I called out to him to stop, when he was about one hundred and forty yards off. I hoped he would stop and give me a broad side, all he did was to look round and as I raised the rifle and fired he dashed at speed across the swamp, and at my second shot, which cut the grass underneath him, he made a most magnificent bound across the stream and disappeared into the wood.

A MOST MAGNIFICENT BOUND.

Another time my brother Richard had gone out after a tiger which the Todas reported had killed a buffalo about an hour before. He saw the tiger on first getting on the ground and the tiger had seen him; he was lying out in the open watching the buffalo, and skulked into the shola and would not come out again. He sat up till twelve and then came home. The next morning Francis started early to reconnoitre, and sent word back to say that the tiger was still there, so away we went. When we got to the ground Francis said the tiger was moving about from rock to rock, and that he had dragged the buffalo into the nullah. We watched for some time without any result; we then went to the edge of the nullah and found that the buffalo had been dragged to the foot of a rock. We crept behind some

THE VULTURES BRING HIM OUT.

bushes and there remained for some time longer, but it was no use, so we decided to go home to breakfast and return in the afternoon. We had got back to the tree where we had previously watched and were on the point of starting home when we observed a number of vultures coming down to the carcass. R. remarked that they would not leave much, when Francis said that the vultures would be sure to bring him out, and he had hardly made the remark when out he came and we could see him quite plain with our glasses; he looked a noble beast. It was a fine sight as we lay watching him; the vultures had all settled down on the side of the hill afraid to go near the carcass. After some time H.R.H. disappeared, and Francis proposed that we should go round and get above the place where we had seen him and watch within shot; in doing so we should disturb the vultures which in all probability would bring him out again. We managed the stalk very well, put the vultures on the wing and got to the edge of the shola, creeping a little further down where we could command all the ground above the buffalo. R. was to have first shot, so I did not even cock my rifle, intending to reserve my fire in case of a charge. The vultures before long began to collect in large numbers on the opposite hill; I counted fifty, but they would not go near the carcass. Several crows more bold came down and kicked up a great row over their meal; all of a sudden they all flew up and I felt certain it was the tiger, but I could see nothing. Some minutes afterwards R. fired. I looked about to see where the tiger was, when R. cried out, "He's dead!" and sure enough on going down there he was as dead as a stone, shot right through the brain, lying just above the buffalo; he had evidently been brought down by the row the crows were making. R. when he fired only saw his ear and part of his head about ninety yards off; it was a splendid shot. Satisfying ourselves that he was dead by pelting him with stones and making a great noise, we went down and inspected him; he was a grand beast. We made him by rough measurement, 9 feet 1 inch long and 3 feet 6 inches at the shoulder. He had a wound four or five inches long and two to three inches deep under his left shoulder, as if cut with a sharp instrument, and it appeared to have been only very lately done.

On the 6th January, 1857, I was out after ibex and sambur. At the little pool of water just beyond the gap on the Sispara road, a sambur had just been having its bath, as the water was quite muddy; I put the people in the little shola beyond but he was not there, and after a long tramp

without seeing any game but plenty of marks both of ibex and bears, I sat down for tiffin on some rocks on the stream at the far end of the great valley. I was reading the *Home News* when I became suddenly aware of something passing in front of me, and on looking up I saw a tiger not thirty paces from me; he was going at a very fast run and took no notice of me, and I doubt if he saw me. I was up in a moment and jumping across the stream, seized the big Laing, but the tiger never slackened his pace, and I only got a snap shot at him as he was going over the spur of the hill about thirty yards off, but the ball arrived at the spot just after he had disappeared; I fancy he must have seen my people as they were all lying asleep in the open.

On Monday, October 5th, 1857, I had an exciting *rencontre* with three tigers. When I came home on Saturday I was informed that one of the elephant keepers had heard

THE MID-DAY SIESTA.

wild elephants that morning in the direction of Pereavai Colum. It was too late to go after them that day, so I decided on going for them this morning, first visiting the bison I had killed in that direction on Thursday, to see if it had been touched by tigers. When we got to the spot we found that the carcass had been dragged out of the high brushwood to a bamboo clump, where it had been half eaten.

A tree close by had the marks of a tiger's claws upon it as high as twelve or fourteen feet. We saw by the marks that there were more tigers than one, and when we got to the nullah at the bottom of the slope, the footmarks were all over the place. Going carefully along it for a short distance, my shikarie made a sign and pointed to a bend in the nullah to the left, and there I saw the striped body of one tiger and part of the body of another. Creeping up to a tree a few paces in front and looking round it, I saw three tigers lying at full length on their backs; they were not above thirty-five or forty paces from me, but there was nothing vital to fire at, as the largest, a tigress, was the farthest from me, and she was lying flat on her back with all her four paws in the air. I could only see her in perspective, and as I was glancing my. eyes over the three dozing beauties, this one suddenly raised her head and stared at me through her four legs. The rifle in my hand was loaded with projectiles and aiming to catch her in the face about the eye I fired. At the report there was a rush and a scrimmage in all directions; the large tigress came tearing towards, but not at me; I waited till she was about twenty or twenty-five paces past me, going like a greyhound, and then fired. A kind of half stumble and a circular swing of her tail proved she was hit, and seizing my big Laing I looked round, and just across the nullah not fifteen paces from me, I saw another tiger looking at me in astonishment; as its body was away from me I let drive at the eye. It sprang forward up the hill, but the second barrel brought it head over heels down again, and catching hold of my spare rifle, I prepared to pitch a three-ouncer into it as soon as it arrived in the nullah, which would have been about six yards from me, but it was stopped by a bamboo clump, upon which I sent the bullet into the point of the shoulder, but, I think, the other shot had killed her; she proved to be nearly a full-grown young tigress seven feet two from nose to top of tail. The third had gone straight up the bank and had got clean away; I then went after the wounded one and found blood immediately beyond where I had taken the running shot and plenty of it.

I knew that it was uncommonly ticklish work following up this tigress which I felt pretty certain was not mortally wounded, but with great caution and a steady hand I trusted to be able to have the best of it if she objected to our proceedings; after some time we came to several places where she had laid down, and as we approached a deep narrow nullah out she rushed along the bottom of it. I had to fire a very snap shot, but it turned her up to the right, and a little further on I saw by the movement of the grass and underwood that she was just in front of us; she had entered another nullah where I soon put her up again; as the ground was not favourable I did not fire; but as she went across through the bamboos I saw she was very badly wounded. It was some time before we again got near her; we had just gone round some thick bushes through which the track pointed and were looking to take it up again, when Atley pointed to some open bamboo jungle, about sixty yards away and there was the tigress lying down looking straight a head; I raised my Ross, took a steady aim and fired, she rolled over on her side never to rise again, but as she kept gasping and showing some signs of life I thought it as well to be on the safe side so put another projectile into her chest. She was a magnificent tigress with a most beautiful skin which I had damaged considerably with the snap shot in the nullah, the ball having played ducks and drakes along her loins. The first shot had broken her right arm near the elbow, the killing shot had taken her in the centre of the neck an inch or two above the shoulder. I made her as she lay without stretching eight feet two inches in length, and three feet two inches at the shoulder. The party had evidently consisted of an old tigress and her nearly full grown children. Got home very tired but uncommonly well satisfied with my day's sport.

On April 13th, 1863, I received a letter from Brooke telling me of an extraordinary adventure. A large solitary boar had been seen and Brooke had been looking after him; late in the evening he met Brine who had been looking out in another direction and who told him that he had come across the old boar face to face in the jungle, but the boar had bolted before he could get a shot and made for the very corner where they were then standing. Just as he had said these words a tremendous grunting was heard and from the shola out bolted the old boar bristling and savage; Brooke was about to raise his rifle when a growl like thunder stopped him and a grand tiger with one spring cleared the nullah and with another lit on the back of the old boar; "such a battle then took place, the growls of the tiger, the grunts of the pig and later, the squeals of the 'sulky one,' made me believe myself in another world. I thought of nothing but killing one or both, so as they were rolling over and over about fifty yards from me on the open hill side, I let fly both barrels; for a second or two the noise went on, and then the tiger jumped off and the boar struggled into the nullah close by. The tiger pulled up and coolly stared at us. Brine took a steady aim, fired, and I believed missed; the tiger still looked at us without moving; but his courage seemed to fail him and he sprang across the nullah into the shola, and disappeared."

One of the most exciting adventures I ever had with a tiger happened in this way. One morning on going to look for a sambur I thought I had wounded, I found the fresh tracks of a leopard or tiger, Francis thought the former, but some of the marks appeared to me too large. As we crossed the opening leading to the upper crags, the lascar pointed to something red in the grass on "bear hill," and on putting up the glasses I saw it was a very large tiger lying down and looking steadily at us: we squatted, and for four or five minutes we remained gazing at one another; he stood up, had a good stare at us and then sat down like a dog. He certainly looked a huge monster, the two white spots over his eyes looked very curious; he was about five or six hundred yards off and there was no getting at him, but at last he slowly rose and stole down towards us into the shola; I think he took us for sambur and intended stalking us. We went to some rocks to meet him, but he never came. I decided on picketing the goats for him, and after fixing on a convenient tree we returned to the hut about noon. Francis at once started with the lascar and the two goats to build a machan; heavy rain set in which did not cease till past four when I went down to see how they were getting on. I made up my mind to remain at the hut all the following week in the hopes of getting this tiger. Francis had built a very good place to watch, and the goats bleated very satisfactorily, but a hind came out and began belling at the goats which frightened them and stopped their noise. I only left the machan when it was too dark to see to shoot. The next morning and all that day the goats remained untouched; on the following morning I sent Francis with the lascar to bring in the goats. The lascar returned reporting that both had been killed and carried off; so after breakfast I went down fully armed. As we approached the spot we heard a curious hissing noise which I thought must be made by a leopard. The blood of the goats were quite fresh, so I

I STARING AT HIM, AND HE GLARING AND GROWLING.

fancied they had only been killed that morning. I took up the track which was not easy to follow; it led into the big shola in the direction in which we had heard this peculiar noise. We had no sooner entered, than a series of low deep growls commenced close by, on our right. It seemed to me as if two tigers were growling at each other, but as there was no tree near available for climbing I was unable to reconnoitre.

We commenced stalking round to get above where the growls came from, and were cautiously creeping up, when Francis suddenly touched me and pointed straight ahead, and there just above us in an open space stood the grand old tiger facing us, growling fiercely and showing his huge yellow teeth—to fire would have been madness, though his broad chest offered a most tempting shot. Francis wanted me to fire, but I whispered, No. I felt if I showed the slightest fear or attempted to retreat he would be immediately upon us, so I tried what steadily staring at him would do. For nearly two minutes we must have remained looking at each other, I staring at him and he glaring and growling and showing his teeth, standing bolt upright all the time, and a grand huge monster he looked; at last he crouched down and opened his eyes wide. I thought he was coming, but knew he could not spring direct from where he was, so if the worst came to the worst I could fire as he approached before his final spring; but I still trusted to the power of the eye, and leaning forward glared at him with all my might; it had the desired effect; he slowly slunk away, and as he turned, his length looked enormous. He crouched so low that his body was almost hidden by the leaves; waiting till he had had time to make himself scarce, I stole up to where he had been, when away he dashed with a growl and a roar not twenty yards from me; I could only see a mass of red, flash through the brush wood.

Whilst looking about for the goat we heard him growling down in the ravine below us, and for a second or two I thought he was coming up towards us; however, I was mistaken. During this adventure both Francis and the lascar had stood by me, but I could see they did not like it, and small blame to them. We found the goat only half eaten, so I sent for the ladder and got up into a tree and watched from 12.30 to 6, but though we were very quiet, the brute was cowed, and he never came back to finish his meal.

Another adventure with a tiger is worth recording. In February, 1867, I was coming home by the bed of a stream, the hills on each side being very precipitous and rocky; at one place there was only a narrow ledge for nearly a hundred yards, and I was just about to proceed along this when my shikarie pointed to a tiger at the further end of the precipitous rocks; he was about a hundred and fifty yards off and standing broadside on, with his head up, looking across the ravine and away from me. I had the carbine in my hand, took a steady aim and let drive; there was a deal of dust and the tiger appeared to twist himself round as if biting at the wound, the next moment he came tearing, tail on end, straight at us along the narrow track. I took the spare rifle from Francis and hastened up the hill so as to be above him; Francis and Muriam instead of following me with the other rifles, bolted straight away over the rocks, right in the tiger's line, to a rhododendron tree and some scanty bushes about fifty yards below. The tiger did not take long getting over the hundred and twenty yards. I had only got a short way up and had wheeled round ready for action, when his head appeared about twenty yards below me; he stopped to look at me and gave two or three nasty puffy snarls and then dashed away down the hill at speed. I now might have had a splendid shot, but he was making straight for the tree behind where I saw the men squatting, and actually passed within eight feet of the boy; as soon as he was clear of the tree I let drive and distinctly heard the ball strike; the beast uttering two or three savage growls, bounded into a strip of shola, throwing up a cloud of dust as he entered. I pitched into Francis and the gun boy for not sticking to

"HE STOPPED TO LOOK AT ME!"

me, especially Francis who ought to have behaved better. We cautiously peered into the shola and found some dirty muddy looking stuff on the grass and leaves; very little of it but the stench was awful, no doubt it came from his intestines. I then crossed the stream and looked into the shola with the glasses, but it was impossible to see far into it; at one time a bunch of dead leaves and fern just outside made my heart beat, it looked so like the tiger lying dead. The strip of shola he first entered was so steep we could hardly get down it; the tiger in his headlong rush had carried everything

WHAT I SAW ONE MORNING.

before him, but further on, the jungle became so thick it was too dangerous to proceed; at one place just below me I could see where he had rolled down, and I was in hopes he had fallen over the precipice. The only thing now to be done was to go home, and come out and look for him later. I went to the spot where he stood when I fired at him, found where the shell had exploded on a rock; but it had first evidently gone through his intestines, for there was more of that most fœtid substance which we had found in the shola. I am pretty certain the tiger did not charge at us, but hearing the explosion of the shell behind him, he had bolted in the only direction left open to him.

One day I was out after a wounded stag and was crossing the hill near Ouna-mund shola when I saw the men making signs to me, and the little dog boy came running up to me saying, "plenty tigers," and pointed down below, and there to my astonishment, down in the valley were five tigers calmly walking across, one of them just leaping over the narrow stream; they went into a small shola, remained there for a short time and then went over the hill into Seven Stag valley, there were two full grown tigers and three young ones the size of large panthers; they were quite unaware of our presence near them.

One day in February, 1868, I was out after sambur when, at some little distance, I saw some hinds and calves standing in a mud pool, looking at what appeared to be a large deer lying down in the swamp some 60 yards from them; on putting my glasses up I saw it was a magnificent tiger who was intently watching them. Suddenly he sprang up and made three or four tremendous bounds towards them, but finding, I suppose, that he could not reach them, he stopped and drawing himself up to his full height remained watching them; presently he slowly came on to an old dry wallowing pool near where the deer had been standing and laid down. The ground was quite open and I hoped he would gradually come up the dip, so I hastened down to meet him, for I was a long way off; when I got to the end of the open ground I took a cautious peep, and saw that he was still on the same spot but with only his head visible; he was a good 200 yards off, and I did not like to take a chance shot at his head or rather part of it, for he had evidently seen me and had crouched; by moving a few paces I could uncover his body, so I put up the 200 yards sight and endeavoured to get a clearer view, but in an instant he was up and bounding away. After going about 50 yards he wheeled round to have a look at me. I fired point blank unluckily forgetting the 50 yards he had gone, and the shell of the carbine threw up the dust right under him making him dash up the hill into the shola at his best pace, more frightened than hurt.

I had shot a bison, a young bull, and had left the carcass on the ground. Two days after as we passed near the spot I turned off to see if a tiger had carried it away, and sure enough the bison was gone; we found it near the nullah. It appeared as if it had only been carried off that afternoon; one hind quarter was nearly demolished, so I determined to watch for the tiger on the morrow. As soon as I arrived at home I had a light bamboo ladder made, as the underwood about was unpleasantly high. The next morning I started with the ladder and my little horse keeper. On approaching the spot we heard the tiger grunting (I cannot use a more expressive term) in the nullah, away on our right. On mounting the ladder I was glad to find the carcass still much in the same place; it had been dragged but a few paces and did not appear to be much eaten. I commenced watching about nine o'clock. At first I sat on the bough of the tree, but in that position I found I could only fire from the left shoulder, so I shifted to the ladder, and having brought the rifle slings I was able to hang the rifles on the bough near me. At first I took my big rifle "Sal," but being afraid the recoil would knock

HE STOOD TO LISTEN, LOOKING THE OTHER WAY.

me clean off the ladder, I changed it for Ross, which was loaded with projectiles. During the watch I noticed several of those large black hornets, with a yellow ring round their bodies, very busy about the carcass of the bison. I had previously seen one of these hornets deliberately robbing the nest of a small kind of wasp, digging out the young larvæ and devouring them with great avidity, the natural guardians apparently looking on at the proceedings of the great robber most apathetically. From this I concluded that the hornets came to feed on the maggots which had become pretty plentiful in the carcass of the bison. After I had been some time on my perch one of those ichneumons, or whatever they are, passed under the tree. I could not get a good sight of it from the branches. It was about twelve o'clock, and I was getting hungry and thinking of tiffin, when I suddenly spied the form of the tiger swiftly approaching the carcass. His quick ear immediately caught the sound of cocking the rifle, and he stood to listen looking the other way; he was partly hidden by bamboos, but his shoulder was quite clear, and he was not above twenty-five to thirty yards off, so I took a steady shot with Ross, to catch him just behind the shoulder. At the report I found myself flying through the air, lighting on my feet at the foot of the ladder, the recoil having knocked me off my perch. I had heard no roar. In an instant I was up the ladder again. No tiger was to be seen. I loaded and went up to the spot; there were the marks of his paws as he had sprung away, and oh! with what a sinking heart I beheld the ground all grooved up by my bullet. I was revived a little when Atley said, after examining the spot, that the ball *must* have passed through the tiger, and was much excited when on the other side of the nullah I found a leaf sprinkled with blood. Cautiously we followed up the track, and I found the ladder of great use, as by mount ing it occasionally I could reconnoitre the whole ground in front. He bled very little, and after about two hundred yards we came to a complete check. After looking about for some time Atley suddenly exclaimed, "He's dead!"

and pointing about twenty yards ahead I saw him lying on his side gathered to his fathers. The ball had gone clean through him behind his shoulders; he was a fine young male but thin and lanky, I could only make him seven feet eight inches as he lay. The next morning I sent Atley to see if any other tiger had been to the Bison, he reported that a tiger had been and had dragged the carcass some yards and had eaten a part of it. I started in the afternoon to watch for him; it was tedious work, but a tiger is worth it. Whilst watching, two of those same animals I had seen previously came, and were scratching up and eating the offal; it was very interesting to watch their ways. At last one of them threw up his nose, and raising himself on his hind legs sniffed about evidently smelling danger, not in my direction, but from where I expected the tiger; it then went up to its companion who was busy at work, and touching it with its nose went through exactly the same manœuvre. The other looked round, sat up and sniffed about for an instant and off they trotted. I fully expected the tiger, but he did not come, and after waiting for three hours and darkness coming on, I went home. It rained the whole of the next day, and when on the following I went to look for the bison, I found that the tiger had been at him, had dragged the remains to the nullah, and nothing but the bones left; rather a bit of bad luck.

On the 12th September, 1868, I was out in the forest that extends along the foot of the Nielgherry mountains looking for any game that might turn up, when I heard a spotted deer give one of their sharp shrill barks; having seen a short time before the quite fresh track of a tiger in the sand of a dry nullah I stole along it, and soon came again on the tiger's track, and then heard another bark of the deer not very far from me. There was a high bank on the side where I heard the sound, with a fallen tree on the top; creeping stealthily along and ascending the bank I peeped over the fallen trunk and my eye instantly fell on the tiger lying in a clump of bamboos, he was broadside on and looking ahead in direction of the deer, lying exactly in the position of one of Landseer's Lions in Trafalgar Square. When tiger shooting on foot I always like to aim at the brain, for then if you do not kill, you know there is no good in following up, whereas if wounded in the body there is always a hope that the animal may be mortally wounded, and more lives are lost following a wounded tiger than in any other way. Unluckily in this case the stems of the bamboos were exactly between me and the back of the tiger's ear, and his shoulder was partly hidden by a tuft of bamboo, so that I could only just see the point of the shoulder; as I was aiming the tiger turned his head and looked straight at me, but it was too late, the next instant he received the bullet. After firing I instantly dropped down under the bank, moved a pace or two on one side and was ready for him if he had come; but on again peering over the bank I had the satisfaction of seeing him lying on his side apparently dead. I say apparently, for these brutes have an awkward way of coming to life again, and in this case he began to struggle, so I slipped a shell into the unloaded barrel and sent a ball into the back of his head and this finished him. But one cannot be too careful, so I waited till I saw the flies begin to settle on his nose and eyes; even then I was cautious, and stealing up behind him I gave a good tug at his tail, and as he did not move I went up and took one of his paws in my hand; it was so flexible it almost made me start. He was a splendid beast in fine condition, having, I afterwards ascertained, killed many a bullock out of the herds that at certain seasons of the year are turned into the forests to graze. His skin when stretched measured nine feet eleven inches; not a particle of his flesh was thrown away, every portion of it was collected, and my men made a good business by selling it at 4d. per pound to the natives, who use it as medicine and who also believe that eating a portion of tiger's flesh will give them the courage of a tiger.

FACE TO FACE.

My friend Drury, when with me at Peer-mund, had rather an exciting meeting with a tiger; he was out one evening after a sambur and was cautiously creeping up to one, when a movement on his left attracted his attention, and suddenly just close in front of him up poked a tiger's head out of the grass, and there they were face to face. No doubt the gentleman in stripes was as much astonished as the gentleman in tweeds, to find his stalk interrupted. On the tiger turning to bolt, Drury let drive at him, and the beast fell dead at the edge of the shola.

The following extract from a letter of the late Colonel Geoffrey Nightingale, a well-known Indian sportsman, will give some idea of the dangers and excitement of shooting tigers from an elephant :—

"In the last year or two I have improved greatly in shooting, especially in steadiness and coolness, which is, after all, more than half the battle, and I find no charge however rapid impairs the accuracy of my aim; I have consequently become, perhaps, foolhardy in allowing tigers to charge up quite close to the huttie ere I fire, and you will see further on how I have (through no fault of my own) reaped the consequence of that over-confidence and very nearly got my dose at last. 'All's well that ends well,' however; and now I doubt anything having the power to make me 'turn a hair.' I can assure you, taking dogs with you when after bison is not such spooney work as you may think; they soon bring a wounded beast to bay and you are certain to be furiously charged directly you come up, so the fun is increased. I don't mean to say I shall make a practice of taking terriers out for bison, but on the occasion I tried it, it answered. I invariably have one or two terriers loose with the line of beaters when after tigers; it makes it much safer for the poor coolies, as my order is, if a dog barks to look out and get up trees, etc., so that I do not run the risk of having my men boned. The other day my line would have come right on a tiger in a thicket had not my dog Crib given warning, when I instantly sent the fellows out of the bushes. Now as to my last week's shikar; having suffered much from fever, this was the first time I was able to go out in February. On the 13th I chulled out forty miles to Morchee, breakfasted, picketed buffaloes and started on my elephant on a chance hunt to a place where Hamilton, the Commissioner, had seen four tigers the week before. I was moving along the bed of a river looking out for anything that might turn up, when Crib gave a bark; I pulled up and saw a commotion in a thick patch of 'jow' (Cyprus) jungle. I suspected it must be some big animal, so told the coolies to go back and spring their rattles; suddenly out rushed two tigers and made off in different directions. I pursued one, a young one, and managed to get in front of him, when he charged me at once; at a dozen paces I managed to put two balls into his chest and upset him, after which I finished him with one under the ear. I then cut away after the second one, a tigress, and could not for a long time find out where she had gone. At last on beating a small ravine off the river, up she got and cantered off; she was hobbling along more than a hundred yards off when I made a very pretty shot with my right barrel and hit her right through the heart; she gave two tremendous bounds into the air, falling on her head each time, and then lay dead. The coolies were flabbergasted at the velocity with which these two brutes were arranged. I then took a beat to explore the ground and put up some pig; they were in a thick thorn jungle, and the ground is generally considered unrideable, but I got on my horse and had a shy, and though I was torn to pieces by the thorns I slew the boar after a couple of charges.

"The next day no buffaloes were killed so I went for a chance beat, only killing a Nilgai. The following day they brought in news that a ghara (a young buff) had been killed; the tiger had only eaten a small portion and then had taken himself off, so I had a long beat without result, but I persevered and struck off to the Nurra river where I had shot the tigers two days ago, and I was lucky enough to put up the beast in a thick patch of grass. Toby barked at him and I saw the tiger running up the opposite bank of the river; a long shot. However, as the jungle beyond was thick and bad, I fired and hit, on which my friend pulled up and lay in some thick bushes, growling at Toby. When I got across the river to the beast, I, not knowing exactly where he was, stumbled right on him; up he jumped and came roaring at the huttie. I gave him two balls, one in the neck, one in the mouth, and upset him, but the plucky beast got up and charged again; he was only five paces off when I fired, and before I could shift my gun the beast had got up to the elephant and had just placed his paw on the elephant's trunk, when I having snatched a gun, leant over and firing close to the mahout's head, rolled the tiger over under the snuffler's trunk just in the nick of time. I was on the top of the hill so a crowd of admiring niggers saw the scrimmage. My elephant is a small one, eight feet odd, and was the staunchest in India I believe; what he may be now I cannot say. This shot just in time was well for the mahout and gave him great confidence, but you will see further on how we were arranged. The day after this was blank.

"Next day a large buffalo of mine was killed; but we could find no tiger, and I beat for hours in vain; however, perseverance is my motto, and I was beating down a ravine towards evening when the tiger was put up; such a whopper. After a long chase I got a running shot at the beast and missed, however, I soon got another point at him and hit him in the shoulder; he rushed off over the brow of a low hill opposite, and suddenly I saw him when about a hundred and fifty yards off charge something in the bushes with an awful roar. I could see nothing, as I knew all the coolies were out of the jungle on a hill and in trees; however, I took a shot and hit, but did not stop the beast, and the next instant I saw to my horror a man emerge from the bushes beyond and walk straight towards the tiger who rushed furiously at him, struck him down and pounced upon him with the evident intention of tearing him to pieces. The tiger and man were in a confused heap on the ground about a hundred and thirty yards off, a very long shot from a huttie; there was a ravine between us, and I could not get closer, I was as likely to hit the man as the tiger if I fired; I was perfectly cool though of course alarmed for the man, and I therefore claim credit for deliberately running the risk of shooting the man and losing my shikar reputation at one blow. It being, however, the poor fellow's sole chance for life, I fired my left barrel with, as it turned out, a good aim. I heard the ball smack loudly, but at such a distance I could not be sure of my shot, but as it sounded like hitting bone I feared it might have hit the man's skull. To my delight the tiger gave a baffled roar, rolled off the man and plunged into the ravine; my conical from the double Kennedy had carried off the entire lower jaw and fangs of the brute. Did you ever hear of such a lucky shot? Anywhere else could not have saved the man, but without a jaw the tiger could not grab him. It is supposed about here that I fired at the jaw, but you and I know better, don't we? It was a cool shot and a good one, but not such a teazer as all that; the man was only wounded behind by the claws, and had not a single bite. I doctored him with arnica, gave him some dibs and sent him off 'whoost.' It turned out he was deaf and was moving about in the jungle. Well, I went after the tiger, and as I got to the edge of the ravine he came at me most furiously; I put a ball right through his neck and he rolled over and ran down the ravine. I cut him off, and the huge beast frantically rushed at me again up the slope; as he came close I gave him my double Kennedy; the first ball in the neck staggered him, the second in the chest slew him on the spot, and he fell with his enormous head over his forearm. He was, indeed, a stunner, with a beard and whiskers like his slayer. Height at shoulder four feet three inches. Length of skin twelve feet eight inches.

"On the following day a report came in that at Lakara there was a noted man-eater, an enormous beast who lived in a den on the hills and could only be got at on foot; he had committed great ravages, taking cattle out of the villages and killing people who went into the jungle, so that no one dare cut grass or wood in his domain. I agreed to have a shy at him on foot, but first I determined to try an 'artful dodge.' Now as my chieftain went out to feed at night I calculated he would not be in his den much before sunrise, so I sent and tied up a buffalo in his jungle and then, starting about 4 a.m. for the hills, got there at dawn, and immediately posted some thirty markers on the peaks of the hills and on trees at each nullah; my plan succeeded, for in less than ten minutes a coolie came rushing up, saying he had seen a 'bagh,' and as I was proceeding to the spot I saw flags waving in every direction all round me. This bothered me a little. I put down my rifle and was making frantic signs to a marker, when out bounded a fine tiger in front of me and was off before I could get hold of my gun. I was now called to come back, so I pulled up and listened, and hearing my dogs Toby and Crib barking, moved the elephant to the spot. It turned out afterwards that the reason for all the clamour on the part of the markers was that I had intercepted no less than five tigers, they having devoured my buffalo, and amongst them was the great man-eater called by the villagers the 'Panura bhag.' On coming up to my dogs, I could not see what they were at, till suddenly my man pointed to a tiger about twelve feet from the ground in the fork of a tree; never expecting him to be up there, I might have gone under him without seeing him. Of course in such a position he had no chance so I put a ball through his heart and giving him one under the ear to prevent revivals I left him hanging, and chulled off the elephant to where I heard loud shouts from the markers above. After going about seven hundred yards as hard as we could lick, a tigress suddenly rushed out of some thick bushes in front of the huttie and went off at full speed; I took a bang at her with the right barrel of the Kennedy and dropped her stone dead with a bullet through the heart; she never even roared. The mahout declared she had gone on but I felt I had killed, and there she was on her back. At this crisis I heard more shouts so started off in their direction leaving the tigress as she lay, and after going nearly half a mile I came to where another tigress not quite full grown was growling at Toby. The mahout pointed her out to me as she sat looking towards me and I dropped her dead with a ball from the double. I now began to think I had got amongst a sounder of tigers, and asked if any more were visible? Oh, yes, was the reply, the Panura has just gone into this valley; so off I started in pursuit of the crusher. After a good deal of beating I put the monster up, and as he ran off gave him a ball behind, missing with my right barrel owing to the elephant moving; some half hour elapsed before I again got a shot at him, but this time as he ran by about one hundred yards off, I put two bullets into his shoulder and he pulled up under a tree. I went up and floored him with four more bullets and he lay at full length apparently dead. I reloaded and was going to give him a pill behind the ear to make quite sure, as he was such an immense beast, but the mahout swore the tiger was dead, so we went up to him and when about fifteen paces from him he suddenly jumped up as if untouched, and rushed at me; at ten paces I gave him the conical in the neck and upset him, but undaunted, this splendid beast dashed on; at five paces I drew the bead between his eyes and pulled the trigger, by Jove! the gun *missed fire*—here was a pretty go.

"Before I could change my gun the tiger came up to the huttie who stood like a rock, and striking him a tremendous blow between the eyes, seized him by the trunk with his teeth and pulled him down on his knees. I was very nearly shot out of the howdah, and what with the mahout roaring that he was being killed (the tiger was close to him, not two inches from his leg), and the man in the khowas screaming 'Saab, Saab,' as we went over, to say nothing of being knocked about like a pea in a rattle, there was enough to confuse me. I am happy to say I never turned a hair, and all my thoughts were bent on flooring the tiger, as I saw that such a monster must otherwise bag us. I managed somehow in the scuffle to put two bullets from a double I had seized, into the brute's back. He let go the trunk and bit the huttie high up on the left shoulder very nearly sending me flying; even in all this confusion, tiger roaring, elephant trumpeting and niggers crying, I shifted my gun, having pitched away the empty one. In the meantime the infuriated demon of a Panura came under the huttie and seized him by the elbow, biting him in the joint high up and pulling him right over on his side. I saw that in another second I should be on the ground, and that it was bag or be bagged, so holding on like grim death to the howdah with my left, I used the gun as a pistol with my right hand, and putting the muzzle close to the tiger rolled him over with a ball between the shoulders. He rushed off with loud roars, but gave the huttie a final cut in the hind leg as he went by. The huttie rose and ran off trumpeting but stopped after a little while: but fancy what had occurred, my scoundrel of a mahout had not brought his 'hankoos' with him so had no command over the animal, who on being told to kneel down became furious, tore up a tree, pitched the mahout off on to the ground and ran off frantically. Well, thought I, this is neat, going like the wind on a mad huttie with no driver. I saw there was but one chance (as I object to jumping off either horse or huttie when run away with, as I always think I can stop him), so unheeding the entreaties of my man in the khowas, I clambered over the front of the howdah, and seated myself on the huttie's neck and tried to drive him; unluckily I had no 'hankoos,' and though I tugged at the brute's ears it was no use as you may fancy; moreover, I found that my spurs were running into his neck and he only went the faster. I therefore after some time got back into the howdah and sat waiting the final smash, which came very soon; for the elephant seeing a large tree made for it and dashed us against it, and I found myself falling from a height of ten feet, howdah and all, backwards; it weighs 250 lbs., so you may fancy the crash with which we came down. The howdah was broken into thirty pieces scattered all round me, the very seat was in bits, yet not a bone had I or my man broken. Did you ever hear of a more providential escape? As I fell, I thought I must be smashed, and after the crash I jumped up amazed but only bruised. I declare I break out into a perspiration when I think of the scrimmage, but then, I was as cool as I ever was. The elephant ran for twenty-two miles, and being bitten and wounded in so many places is not yet well enough to be brought in. Well, after picking up the pieces, I felt as you may suppose somewhat riled with my friend the Panura; so as I felt sure he must be very seedy, if not actually dead after so many balls, I reloaded my guns and walked to the spot where the fight had taken place, as I was not going to be done by him. We advanced very cautiously as you may fancy; at last we saw his outline in the grass about fifteen yards off, and telling my people to keep steady I fired into the heart—no row, so up I rushed with a yell, and the man-eater of Lakara was my own. Oh! such a sniffler! Height at shoulder, four feet two inches; length of animal, ten feet two inches; length of skin, twelve feet six inches. His fangs were exactly four of my fingers in length; as he was brought in, whole villages turned out and abused him. So ended my trip: in six days I bagged eight tigers, two nhilgie and a boar. It will be some time before I can have another shy at tigers, and probably my elephant is ruined, as no huttie can face a tiger again after such a mauling. His trunk was bitten through in a dozen places."

THE LEOPARD. (*Felis pardus.*)

The leopard, or as he is often called in Southern India, the cheeta from the native word *chita*, is a most beautiful animal to look at. Some naturalists assert that we have two species of leopards independent of the true cheeta, in India; the panther, and the tree leopard: for my part I never could tell the difference, which I believe is chiefly in the size, the larger leopard being sometimes almost as large as a tigress. McMaster agrees in this and believes that there is only one species, and that varieties in colour, shape, and size, are accidental or caused by climate or diet.[1] The leopard is a very formidable animal to meet; from being much bolder and more active than the tiger he is exceedingly dangerous, and although he cannot kill with one blow as the tiger does, I have known several instances where lives have been lost or persons very fearfully mauled by leopards. Sir James Outram who was as great a sportsman as he was a soldier, told me that he would sooner any day face a tiger than a leopard.

The leopards are often found up among the branches of trees, and they run about them with the activity of a squirrel. They are very fond of preying on the large black monkey,

---

[1] Blandford (Fauna of British India) makes only one species *Felis pardus*, the Leopard or Panther.

and they often lie crouched on a low branch ready to drop on some unlucky deer or wild hog that may pass under it. Coming home one day from shooting in the bush I noticed at the foot of a tree some very fresh rootings of wild hog and said to my man, there must be a pig about here. As I spoke I heard a rustle in the leaves above me, and the next moment a leopard's head appeared level with mine on the

I COULD HAVE SLAPPED ITS FACE.

stem of the tree. It was so close I could have slapped its face, but before I could get my rifle to the shoulder he was on the ground and hidden by the jungle. Their tenacity of life is very great; I have known a leopard after remaining as if dead for more than half an hour, spring up and tear up the grass all round him. On one occasion after knocking

THE JUNGLE CAT (Felis chaus).

over a leopard, I left it apparently quite dead; on returning some time after, I was surprised to find it was gone, when I suddenly saw it a short distance away with its back up looking awfully fierce, and the next moment I fully believe it would have charged me had I not effectually put a bullet behind its shoulder. This shows how careful one ought to be in approaching any of these big cats, supposing them to be dead. Even the common wild jungle cat (*Felis chaus*) of Southern India is an awkward customer at times. It is a tall long legged, short tailed animal, almost as unlike our domestic cat as the wild dog is to its civilized brother. One of these cats came into our cantonment evidently on the prowl for fowls or anything it could pick up, so we collected all the dogs we could, and had a hunt; after some time we found it, and a very exciting chase we had amongst the hedges that divided the officers' quarters. We came to a long check, the dogs being quite at fault; after looking about for some time I spied the cat squatting in a hedge and called for the dogs; when they came, I knelt down and began clapping my hands and cheering them on; the cat suddenly made a clean spring at my face; I had just time to catch it as one would a cricket ball, and giving its ribs a strong squeeze I threw it to the dogs, not however before it had made its teeth meet in my arm just above the wrist; for some weeks I had to carry my arm in a sling, and I shall carry the marks of the bite to my grave.

I have not killed many leopards although I have often come across them both on the ground and in trees, but they are so crafty and sly that it is very difficult to get a fair shot at them. It was when out after ibex that I mostly met with them, as they are particularly partial to the flesh of this animal and prefer it to all other food. It will sit and watch on a crag above its prey (knowing well that the ibex never looks up), until the opportunity comes for the fatal spring. But a young calf sambur or even a full-grown deer does not come amiss to them. I once killed a sambur from the

IT WILL SIT AND WATCH ON A CRAG.

shoulders of which a leopard had only a few minutes before torn a mass of flesh.

I was fortunate once in slaying a very fine black leopard. On the 16th May, 1857, I left the hut just as dawn was appearing, having sent the guns and people on ahead. I took the road to the coffee plantations, and was just going round to the ibex rocks, when happening to look back I saw something black on the rock on the low hills behind me; on looking with my glass to my delight I saw it was a black leopard. He was capitally situated for stalking owing to there being some higher rocks behind him, but I was doubtful as to the

THE BLACK LEOPARD.
"He was not more than fifty yards and lying down."

wind, and as I was working round, to my great disappointment I saw him move off the rock; hastening up I found that he had only moved a little more to the left and was still on the same rock. He was not more than fifty yards from me, and was lying down; all I could see of him was his head, neck, and back; he was looking away from me. I felt rather unsteady in my aim, so took a long time about it, and when I did fire, had the pleasure of seeing him fall on his side bent up

15

in a convulsive spasm. He gave one or two struggles and then disappeared over the rock. On going up I found it was the edge of a precipice, and on looking down saw him lying

THE BLACK LEOPARD—HIS DEATH.

dead some eighty feet below me; a beautiful animal as black as the blackest tom cat, and when put in the light, one could see the dark spots all over him. The bullet had struck higher than I anticipated, entering through the back part of the ear, traversing the brain and passing through the opposite eye. The black variety is scarce in Southern India. I only saw one other during all the years I was on the hills.

I had the misfortune to lose one of my best dogs from the bite of a leopard. I was coming home after having been all out the morning, a heavy mist had set in and I did not know where I was till I found myself in Kereká Valley. I put the dogs through a little shola just above; the mist was so thick I could not see above a dozen yards, and no sooner were the dogs in than I heard a half yelp, half scream, and the dog boy called out "Sahib, there's a tiger." I hastened to the top of the wood, where I found Bevis barking loudly, but disinclined to go in again; presently I heard a noise as of a jungle fowl flying up into a tree, which made me think that the scream I had heard was made by a monkey and that Snob was busy with the jungle fowl; on calling and whistling I heard a low sound—what I took to be pigeons. Alas! on listening attentively I found it was the moaning of poor Snob. Taking the big Laing and telling the lascar to follow closely with the other rifle, I forced my way through the tangled jungle; as I was making my way down the dog began yelling as if the "Bhag" was on him again, so I fired off the rifle and shouted lustily. I soon found the poor dog lying on his back frightfully mauled about the head and his brain protruding through one bite just above the ear; he was also bitten through the neck and shoulder, and from the bites I saw at once that a leopard had been at him. Putting the poor dog in a cumbly I hastened home, and as I came to the little shola, close by the pool of water, I saw the fresh track of a large sambur, and on ahead in the mist saw what I at first thought was a Toda buffalo lying down facing me; as the mist cleared a little I saw it was a stag, so knocked him on his side with a ball in his chest, and as he rose gave him another behind the shoulder and Bevis pinned him. On going up I found that the deer had also been in the leopard's

THE LEOPARD'S RIDE.

clutches; there was a frightful wound under the elbow, all the muscles and flesh torn out, and his back and flank torn from end to end by the beast's claws. How the deer had got rid of its enemy it is difficult to say, but the stag must have had an unpleasant time of it while it lasted. Poor Snob died the next day.

The following account of a fight with a cheeta is taken from the journal of 1838:—

Upcher of the fifty-first, started out snipe shooting this morning with my gun. He had not gone far, when he met Colonel J., who told him that there was a leopard in the cave in the rocks, close to the lines of the regiment. Upcher, who is always ready for a bit of sport, immediately took the shot out of the barrels of the gun and put in ball and sallied forth with J. and a young fellow, T—— by name. . . . The latter was placed on the top of the rock whilst Upcher and J. walked up to the mouth of the cave, which had two entrances. They could not see the leopard at first, but on getting a little higher on the rock, Upcher caught sight of it and fired. The beast at once rushed out and ran behind a large rock. They both made after him, Colonel J. following the cheeta's path, while Upcher went round the other way so as to meet it, which he pretty soon did ; and the moment the leopard caught sight of him, he came slap at him. Upcher jumped two or three paces one one side and fired. The shot only staggered the brute, and Upcher at once tried to make off, but before he could turn round the leopard was almost upon him. Seeing now that it all depended on his presence of mind, activity and strength, he struck the animal with the gun with all his force as the leopard was in the act of striking him, and so warded off the blow from his head and only received a severe cut on his right cheek from the beast's claws from one paw, the other at the same moment striking the gun and sending it clean away. Upcher then put his right hand into the leopard's mouth, and with the other hand grasped him tight round the throat. The brute as soon as he found that Upcher had got him by the throat, let go of his hand and caught him near the elbow; Upcher still keeping his hand and part of the forearm in the mouth. By this time they had struggled close to two rocks, which had a rift between them, and Upcher by main force threw the leopard on his back into it—keeping his knee on his chest—his right hand in his mouth, and his left still tight round the animal's throat. At this moment Upcher's boy came up with a double-barrel gun. Upcher told him to put the barrels into the leopard's mouth and fire. The bold little fellow obeyed him, pulled both the triggers and blew the beast's brains out, fortunately missing injuring the hand, which was fearfully mauled by the fangs, every finger being lacerated and the hand bitten through; the forearm was also bitten in five places, and his left hand and arm were much injured. During this fearful encounter T. was standing on the rock with a double-barrel gun loaded with ball simply looking on. There were also half-a-dozen natives on the rock, but none went to the rescue, and if it had not been for the gallant little boy, Upcher must have been killed. The leopard was a large male, and on examination the ball from Upcher's gun had passed through the lower part of the chest, cutting the tendons of the heart. My gun is very much damaged, I believe, but I have not seen it yet.

I was out after deer one windy morning near Peer-mund, and was watching a sambur with only one antler. I had sat down on a ledge of rocks and, just as I was moving away, I saw a leopard stealing through the grass about twenty yards below me. I clucked for him to stop, but the wind was too high for him to hear me, and he would have been out of sight in a second or two, so I let drive at him as he was stealing through the grass like a snake; he was evidently after the stag. As the ball struck him he bounded clean round, when I threw him on his tracks with the second barrel; on going down to him I saw he was still breathing, and as he was lying close to the edge of a precipice I did not like to fire another shot for fear of sending him over. I waited for more than a quarter of an hour; rolled some stones over him, but he did not move or take any notice of my shouting at him. Still, I did not like to go too close to him. At last, as his breathing appeared to improve, I took a shot at him with the carbine at about fifteen yards, and to my astonishment he jumped up and commenced tearing at a tuft of grass with his claws, when I at once settled him with a ball in the brain; he was an old male with his lower tusks all broken and worn down, but his skin was very glossy and in good order. I could only make him six feet three inches from nose to tip of tail.

One has disappointments when least expected. One day when out after game I ought to have killed two leopards, but I did not, and this was how it happened. My friend, Tom Clarke, a superstitious fellow, would have laid it at once to my meeting two hares. I had had rather a long trudge, and had gone over a deal of ground only seeing these two hares, when I came across a path where a leopard had dragged some animal; following it up, I found the carcass of a calf fresh killed with only one leg eaten. Shortly afterwards I heard some animals moving in the thick jungle ahead. As I expected from the sound, they were bison. I managed to knock over a big old bull and a cow, and having cut out their tongues and amputated the cow's tail for soup, I reached the tent between eleven and twelve, and began to think that Tom Clarke's theory of the hares was not always correct, and that they at times brought good luck. Whether he or I was right the sequel will show. Francis was convinced that the leopard would not come to the calf after all the firing and the noise the people would make on going for the bison, so he wanted me to take some other ground in the evening, but I fancied the leopard might come, so after salting the tongues and writing a letter I started about 5 p.m., on the chance. I found the leopard had dragged the calf to the bank of the stream, and into some bushes so thick that there was no chance of getting a shot unless we could get to the other side of the nullah. After losing our way, we at last hit the spot where we had been in the morning, and as we approached we heard the leopard give a snarling growl, I was then in the bed of the nullah on a kind of island studded with high trees,

THE STAR IS WHERE THE BALL STRUCK.

and on the opposite side of the stream was a high bank with trees on the top of it. With eager eyes I looked up and down and along the opposite bank, but could see nothing, when suddenly I saw something on the thick branch of a tree on the top of the opposite bank some sixty paces off. It was getting rather dark, and at first I could distinguish nothing but a round knob on the branch, with two projections that looked uncommonly like a pair of ears; another look and I saw it was a leopard's head, for I could plainly see its white teeth as it opened its mouth at me. I took a steady shot at the brute's head, for nothing more could I see. There was a crack which I had hoped was from bones, but the creature was up in an instant and ran along the branch like a squirrel, and bounding down disappeared in the jungle in less time than I can write it. All my hopes vanished when I saw the mark of my shot on the branch. I was so afraid of firing over, that, alas! I aimed a trifle too low. Francis had not seen the animal until it moved from the spot. I re-loaded, and while we moved a few paces towards the stream, was discussing with Francis the possibility of the ball having gone through the leopard's jaw, when I fancied I saw a movement in a branch near the top of a tree under which we had been standing. By Jove, it was another leopard! the brute stopped for a moment, but was so hidden by leaves and branches that I waited for a better chance, but alas, that never came; it ran down the branch like lightning, never showing but an inch or two of its back. I got one glimpse of its head and neck and fired. The next moment it had bounded on the high bank and disappeared in the thicket. As I expected we could find no signs of either having been touched; Francis said the second was a "butcha," it looked small—and so did I, uncommonly, to see a brace of leopards getting away from me with whole skins, for I would much rather have bagged one of these than the two bison. The recollection of the two hares in the morning suddenly flashed across me, and then I knew how it was my bullet went crooked. Tom Clarke is right; blow the hares! But perhaps it was for the best, for if I had bagged these two leopards under the circumstances I should have been an unbearably conceited beast ever afterwards; but it would have been a great thing to have killed these cattle-destroying brutes, to say nothing of my limited bag in this line. It was getting dusk, so had only time to look into the bush where we had seen the calf. It was not there; oh, if I had come down to watch at once, I must have got one of them.

As I came home across the paddy bunds I lost my footing, I had already lost my temper!

When at Naadgarmee on 8th February, 1870, I went out at sunrise to search the precipices in the rear of the camp for ibex, but saw nothing. In the afternoon out again with Francis; it had been very misty all day and the fog was still hanging about the precipices; when we got near them I saw something move on a rock about one hundred and twenty yards from me; I knew it was a leopard by the way it crouched on seeing us. From being very misty I fancy it could not make us out; and as we were looking at it with the glasses it suddenly glided out of sight, but appeared on the hill again almost immediately, rather nearer to us, and I thought for a moment it had taken us for deer or ibex. It then returned to the rock looking so dark that I thought is was one of the black variety and the mist magnified it considerably as it stood, looking so handsome; it again disappeared over the rock which was close to the edge of a precipice. I fancied I saw another head on the same rock which vanished at the same time, and I stalked up to a small tree about sixty yards above the rock. I had not waited long when the leopard again appeared, facing me; I think he saw me but he was quite distinct as he stood on the edge of the precipice, so I took a steady pot at him, a loud thud and the beast was head down and tail up. Francis was delighted and cried out, "all right, he's dead," and was going down to him, but I prevented him. We both thought there was another close at hand and as we were working round to get above the one lying stretched on the grass, apparently as dead as Julius Cæsar, I suddenly saw the head and neck of another within twenty yards of me looking at its fallen companion. Before I could raise the rifle the animal disappeared over the precipice; I at once ran to the edge and waited some time with the hope of seeing it again, but after about twenty minutes—Francis says half an hour—I went back towards the dead leopard and got to about thirty paces from him when, to our utter astonishment, up he sprang and bolted towards the edge of the rock; I fired a quick shot with a shell and the leopard disappeared in a narrow water course close to the precipitious side of the rock. I felt pretty certain I had hit him, and thought I had heárd a stifled growl; cautiously approaching the spot I had the satisfaction of seeing him lying dead; had he gone another yard he would have been over the edge. I found my first shot had hit him on the right nostril knocking his teeth about and passing out behind the jaw; why he should have remained stunned for so long a time I can't make out. The shell had entered high up behind the left shoulder, passing out and smashing the right, dropping him dead on his tracks; he was an old male six feet two inches in length with a beautiful skin.

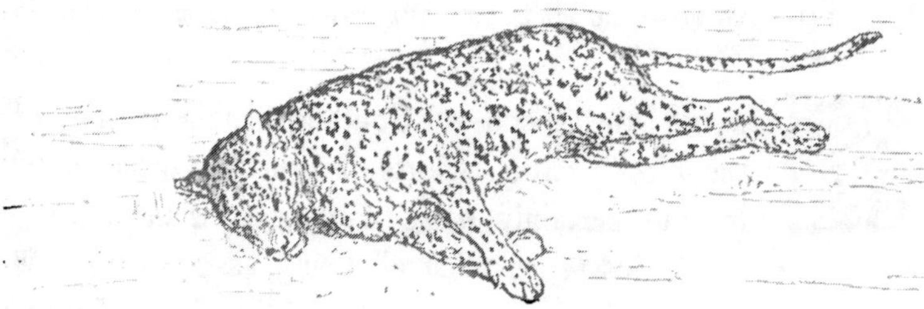

MY LAST LEOPARD.

HEAD OF A BULL BISON.

CHAPTER IX.

BISON.

THE BISON OF SOUTHERN INDIA—SIZE OF THE OLD BULLS—DANGER IN STALKING THEM—COL. CAMPBELL'S MISNOMER—LARGE HORNS—MY FIRST BISON—ADVENTURE WITH OLD EMAM—WOUND AND LOSE AN ENORMOUS BULL—MORE LUCKY WITH THE NEXT—A GRAND FIGHT WITH ANOTHER—CAPTURE A SMALL CALF AND TAKE HIM HOME—NO MORE BULLETS—MY LAST RESOURCE—VERY MUCH ASTONISHED ON BOTH SIDES—A TALL SHOT AT A BULL AT SPEED—NOT THE PLEASANTEST MOMENT OF MY LIFE—A NARROW ESCAPE—A BIG BULL STOPS THE WAY—MY LAST BISON—THE BIG BULL OF PEER-MUND.

STALKING the Bison of Southern India is one of the most exciting sports imaginable, quite equal to and certainly more dangerous than hunting the wild elephant, his sense of smell being as great and his organs of vision much more acute. The sight of one of these grand bulls in his native wilds with his head erect and his eye glistening with anger as he scents danger is an object not to be forgotten. The rush of a wounded bison through the jungle as he crushes down the saplings and the bamboos is quite appalling, and the crafty manner in which he will wait for you, when following his bleeding tracks, hidden in some high grass, is enough to make the most daring proceed with the greatest caution, for a toss from an enraged wounded bull is pretty certain to bring you to the utmost grief. The solitary bulls are the easiest to approach, but they are also the most dangerous. It is strange how easily they can hide themselves in the jungle; I have been within twenty paces of a big bison, hearing him snuffle, seeing the grass move, and yet he remained quite invisible. If a herd, particularly when feeding happen to get your wind, they make themselves scarce in no time, and will disappear as if by magic.

The GAUR, *Gavæus gaurus*, Jerdon. *Bos gaurus* of other authors; is known to all sportsmen of Southern India as the Bison; why Col. W. Campbell should state that Madras sportsmen call this animal a wild bull, except that the male is a bull and is wild, is incomprehensible. It is certainly the largest of all existing bovine animals. The males average from five feet eight to five feet ten in height, and the cows from five feet to five feet three, but at times monsters of both sexes are met with. I have killed bulls measuring six feet at the shoulder, and I once killed a cow bison measuring five feet eight inches. An old bull bison is a magnificent animal, the normal colour is a brownish black, sometimes in very old specimens almost quite black, and then the white stockings from the hoof to above the knee are very conspicuous. The horns of the bulls are grand trophies, the average may be from twenty to twenty four inches round the outside curve but many are much larger. The figure below is the skull of a bison shot by Lt. Burnside, at Dindegal, the outside curve being thirty-two and a half inches. The big bull of Peermund, the last bison I killed had one of his horns broken, but the sound horn was thirty-five inches long and eighteen inches in circumference at the base. The largest horns of a cow bison I killed were twenty-five and a half inches in length, and nearly twelve inches in circumference at the base.

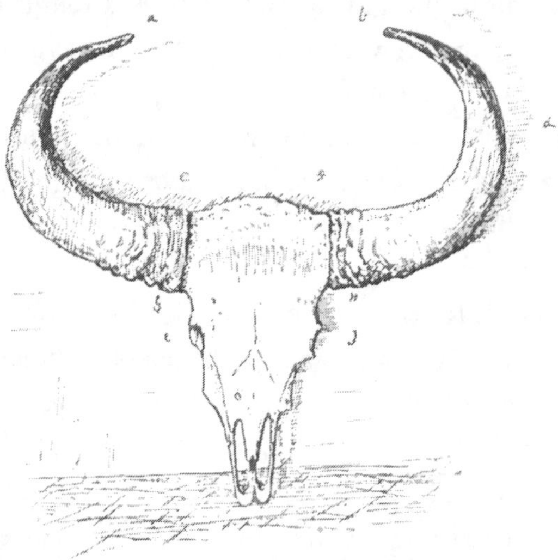

DIMENSIONS OF THE HORNS.

a. to b. 25½ inches
c. to d. 42 inches
e. to f. 12½ inches over the ridge
e. to g. }
f. to h. } 17 inches in circumference

i. to j, 10½ inches
Length of R. horn 32½ inches outer bend
Length of L. horn 31½ inches
Length of head 22¾ inches.

The first bison that fell to my rifle was in my trip to the Dandilly forest, he was a young bull. I had some rather stirring adventures with them, but at that time I was young, and much too excitable to be a steady shot; one of these adventures is worth recording. One evening I went with

Emam the shikarie, to where Watson (my companion) had shot a bull the day before; we waited till near sunset before entering the likely ground; the wind was blowing strong and the old man entered the valley down wind very much to my surprise. I fancied I heard a bamboo crack, and on looking in the direction saw a bison trotting away, he had been feeding in a clump of bamboos about fifty yards from us, but getting our wind took to his heels. Old Emam was disgusted at his oversight, but almost immediately spied another lying down in the middle of a dense jungle of bamboos; as Emam pointed him out to me he rose; he was about thirty-five yards off and stood breast on. The bamboos were so thick and close together that I could only see a great black mass; I had to guess where the middle of his chest was and let drive; down he fell on his knees, but instantly rose again and advanced one or two steps towards us (Emam told me afterwards that he was going to charge). I gave him the other barrel and down he came again, but was soon up again and began shaking his enormous head very indignantly. I took my spare gun; I was quite cool, so much so that when I found I was not covering him properly, I put it down and brought it up again and fired. Emam declared I had missed; whether I did so or not, it sent him to the right about and he bolted, I gave him the other barrel and am certain I heard the tell, but the bamboos were so close together that nearly every shot had to cut its way through them. I reloaded as fast as I could and dashed on after him; we soon came on his blood, and Emam pulling up said, "this is an immense bison, if he charges get instantly behind a tree, or you are a dead man." I looked round; we were in the midst of a male bamboo jungle so thick that we could scarcely see twenty yards ahead, and the few trees were scattered fifty to sixty yards apart. It would be impossible to run ten yards without falling, on account of the young bamboos and other creepers (broken down by the bison feeding) lying on the ground so interlaced that they would be certain to get entangled between our legs and trip us up; but in the excitement of the moment, the dangers of the situation appeared mere trifles to me, and on we went, not making the slightest noise for fear of bringing the enraged monster on us, Emam making certain that everything that looked black was not the bison, before he proceeded a step. Some of the bamboos were covered with blood, and the beast was evidently so badly wounded that he could not face the opposite hill; we came to where he had attempted it and had turned back to keep along the valley. At last the jungle getting much thicker, the trees fewer, and the sun having set for some time, Emam stopped and said we should certainly find him a little further on, but as certainly he would charge us if he was not too far gone, and as in such a jungle we could not possibly get out of his way, unless he was dropped in the charge, one or both of us must be killed. It was getting dark and we might come upon him at any moment before we knew it, and if so, and he was alive, there would be very little chance for us. So taking all these things into consideration, I turned away with a sad heart, leaving the finest bison I had seen severely, probably mortally, wounded. I asked Emam if Watson and I went together the next morning with the shikaries carrying all our spare guns we should have a chance of finding him.

He said the jungle was so thick that we could only advance in single file, that one man was as good as fifty, and the bamboos being very thick would prevent any one firing to the right or left, so I gave up all hopes of getting him. I afterwards offered Emam twenty rupees if he would bring him in; he said he would try if I promised to pension his family in case he was killed. Emam told me that bison always charge with their heads up until they approach close to you, so that when the jungle is all open it is easy enough to get out of their way. Since that time, many a grand bull has fallen to my rifle; I will take a few of the best stalks from my Journal.

When on the Annamullies I had a grand fight with a big bull. I was out early, and came on the spoor of bison, and soon saw two, one a very large bull; to my disgust he laid down and was completely covered by a lot of creepers and bushes. After a bit I attempted to move to get a better view; but there to my left .was a cow staring at me; she at once gave the alarm, and I waited for the large bull to rise; this he did so very rapidly, and disappeared so suddenly that I only got a snap shot, but I thought I heard a tell. As I stopped to load I saw a young calf squatting at the foot of a tree like a hare, intently watching me. I put the rifle down, crept up behind the tree, and suddenly threw myself upon the little brute and laid hold of one of its hind legs, but it got from under me. I managed, however, to tie its forelegs with my handkerchief; all this time it continued to bellow and kick up a great row, and I fully expected the mother to come charging down, but it appeared that fear was greater than affection, and I managed to bind its legs securely, by means of some slender stems of the creepers. I went back to the bungalow and sent some men to bring my captive home. After breakfast I started again, accompanied by Atley and another man to take up the track of the bison. We soon got on it, but were delayed by a heavy shower; when it was over Atley showed his "cuteness" by cleverly keeping the true track, and he became very excited when, after half an hour or so, we came on the foot marks not filled with water, and then we suddenly caught sight of the bison just ahead. As we crept on expecting every moment to come upon them, I heard a strange noise to my left; I asked what it was, and Atley made use of a word I did not know, but from the sound I thought it was a tiger. We turned off in that direction, and I fully expected to come upon the "gentleman in stripes;" I saw some branches move, and on carefully looking perceived a very large bull bison instead, he was amongst thick bushes, and I could only see an indistinct outline. I guessed as near as possible the position of the shoulder and fired the big rifle at him, he gave a bound forward and then stopped sufficiently long for me to give him another shot from the double rifle; he then dashed onwards, but I had heard the thud. We followed the spoor for some distance without finding a drop of blood, and Atley gave me a most reproachful look, but the next moment I pointed to a bamboo quite red with blood, and just beyond we saw the bull standing on the high ground above us. I fired and hit him well behind the shoulder, but he dashed off, only, however, going about fifty yards, when he stopped, and I walked down to him thinking to give him the finishing shot with my big rifle "Sal"; suddenly he made a fearful rush at me. Atley put the double into my hand and bolted, and I thought it prudent to retire and bide my opportunity; he only moved forward a few paces and then stopped, and now commenced a regular siege. I advanced and the enemy retired behind a tree, but I could see the cunning rascal with his ears well forward waiting for me to come on. I crept up to about thirty paces and as I could only see his head, I thought I would give him a three ounce ball between his eyes which I did, but it only sent him to the right about. I again advanced and again found him waiting for me, so I planted another bullet much in the same place; this immediately pro-

I PLUNGED MY HUNTING KNIFE INTO HIS SIDE.

duced a furious charge, and I was obliged quickly to retire behind the trees, giving him a side shot as he turned; he then laid down, and I tried to knock him up with a bullet behind the shoulder and to knock him down with another behind the eye; I succeeded in the former, but not in the latter, though I put the ball into him exactly where I aimed. I now had only one bullet left; I went close up, and watching my opportunity placed it low down behind the shoulder, he fell, but was up again in no time and tried to get at me, but I was up the hill above him, and he was too much done to charge effectually. He presently laid down, and not having a bullet left I was reduced to the waiting game; he got up again and tried to charge, but after going a few paces laid down and rolled over on his side. I thought he was dead, but what was my astonishment when he again got up on his legs and quietly walked off, and when he laid down again it was as naturally as if he had not got a single hole in his skin. This looked pleasant; I did not like to leave him and I had only one resource, so I tied my hunting knife to a long bamboo and creeping up plunged it into his side just under the elbow. This finished him; he was a very large bull over six feet in height, with magnificent horns. Atley compared him to an elephant, and indeed some of these big bulls take more killing than most elephants. On arriving at home I found the little calf standing in the verandah, and it allowed me to pat it without showing the slightest fear, it was such a pretty little thing.

One morning I was out after elephants and had been following them for a long time, but the herd had moved on some distance, so I bivouacked for tiffin, choosing a place by the side of a small stream, with a high bank on the other side, and opposite where I sat, was a well worn track with marks of deer, bison, and pig. I took the precaution to have the light rifle within reach. I had had my tiffin and was reading the "Athenæum," when I suddenly heard a snort and on looking up I beheld on the top of the opposite bank a big bull bison staring at me. I was much astonished, but I carefully laid down the "Athenæum" with one hand and took up the rifle with the other, the bison standing all this time perfectly still as if wrapt in amazement; but just as I pulled he made a quarter turn and the ball hit him somewhere about the front of the shoulder which stopped him for a moment, giving me time enough to fire the other barrel. We packed up traps as quickly as possible and followed him, soon came to blood, and had just come to a check when we were all startled by the loud roar of an elephant close by. So

"A BIG BULL BISON STARING AT ME."

all thoughts of the bişon were given up and away we went after the roarer.

One day in 1856 I made rather a tall shot at a bull bison. I was out with Michael and whilst exploring the forest to show a friend a full sized teak tree, we came upon the fresh tracks and soon after upon a herd of bison, but they winded us and were off, Michael getting a quick shot and bagging a cow. After tiffin, on our way to the horses we came upon another herd. Michael went ahead, I was standing still when Atley ran up and touched me, making a sign that some of the herd had turned back, and taking the Ross rifle, I ran up just in time to intercept a bull and a cow; I gave the former, one barrel as he stood and the other as he dashed at speed across a bit of open, which brought him down with a tremendous crash as dead as a stone, he was a small bull but with good horns.

WITH A TREMENDOUS CRASH AS DEAD AS A STONE.

I had a most exciting encounter with bison one morning. Soon after entering the forest I heard the twigs breaking near us, but the beasts either smelt or heard us; a couple of snorts, a rush and they were gone. We took up the tracks of what appeared to be a large bull and a cow; got quite near them, but again came the snorts and they were off; again we came up to them, and I saw a small cow, but at the same time got a glimpse of a huge mass behind her, which made me wait, as I was certain it was an immense bull by the size of the footmarks; another snort and another rush, and they were off a third time. We found now that there were five of them—with two thundering big tracks of two huge bulls, so I determined to follow them, and after a good long chull again came in sight of them. I saw the body of one of the big ones standing broadside on about sixty paces off, so I let drive, and as it rushed away, knew I had hit from the quantity of blood flowing, and had the satisfaction of seeing, from the footmarks, that it came from one of the big bulls. We had not gone far before we found it lying dead. The other big bull was just behind a bamboo clump; I moved on one side to get a fairer shot, and just as I pulled the trigger it snorted and bolted, Atley declaring I had made a hit. We went back to the dead one, and to my astonishment found it was a cow; the largest I had ever seen, and with the largest horns. After taking the tongue, we took up the track of the bull, about which there could be no mistake this time, for there were the footprints, so much larger than the others. There was a great quantity of blood at first but it gradually lessened till there was only a drop or two here and there; we had a long track and at last just as we got into the thick bushy underwood and amongst the young teaky looking stuff we heard the bison rush away close in front, but the bush was too thick to see through; following as best we could, we heard it breathing heavily a little beyond us. I was in this dense underwood and was in the act of creeping through it to get in front of the animal when I suddenly heard a rush to my right and the bison was upon me with its head down between its forelegs. I attempted to turn or rather spring on one side and get the rifle to bear, when I fell! I thought it was all over with me; but the big brute passed clean over me, and, oh! how thankful I felt when I found I had got off with only a severe bruise on my right leg just below the calf, probably from one of the feet hitting me as it passed. We followed up the track but were more cautious than before expecting every moment to be charged, and after some time we heard the heavy breathing

Not the pleasantest moment of my life.

30th August 1856

again in the same kind of thick jungle. We crept round, or rather I did, for it wanted some coaxing to get Atley to follow; got on a fallen tree and looked cautiously in every direction, but could see nothing, although still hearing the heavy soughing of the beast. I crept on from tree to tree and had just told Atley to send for the dog as I was determined to have the brute if I waited till dark, when I suddenly spied a bison's ear about twenty paces off cocked towards me.

Judging where the root of that ear must be, I took a steady shot and the bison was arranged, but as I could still hear it breathing I stole up and killed it with a shot behind the ears. To my intense disgust and chagrin, instead of finding a magnificent pugnacious old bull, there was a cow! and not a very large one either, but her feet which had so misled me, were bigger than almost any bull I had ever tracked. The other cow was nearly seventeen hands high, with horns twenty-five and a half inches long and handsomely curved, sixteen inches across and nearly twelve in circumference.

One day when out after elephants, and on the track of a big tusker, a fine bull bison, walked out of some low bushes right in our way. He stood about twenty yards from us, and not seeing us commenced rubbing his horns against a tree; such a chance one don't often get when out after bison. I clapped my hands, as there was no time to lose. On this he looked up, and on my throwing up my arms, he tossed his head, and showed such an inclination to charge that Atley fairly halted. Again I threw up my arms and again he put his head down and shook it at me. Not wishing to fire, which I must have done if he had charged, I retreated, upon which he obligingly did the same.

I was told that a very large bull bison had been seen in the sholas about Peer-mund, and on the 19th Nov., 1866, having been out since earliest dawn after sambur, of which there was hardly a trace to be seen, probably owing to the wild dogs having hunted them out of these woods last year. When outside the shola, at the foot of "the stag hill," I saw a bull bison lying down; made a good stalk through the shola and got about fifty yards from him; he was lying down on the hill above me. I took a steady aim as near the ground as I could and fired. At the shot he rose with difficulty, and while doing so I gave him the other barrel. He walked to the edge of the shola, about thirty yards distance, stood for a moment just inside, and then fell with a crash, stone dead. A very fine old bull, but unfortunately one horn had broken in half. I made the good horn thirty-three inches long and eighteen inches in circumference; the meet would have been about forty inches had the horns been perfect. A grand head, indeed; what a pity! This was the last bison I killed.

A DEAD BULL.

THE SÁMBUR.

CHAPTER X.

THE SAMBUR AND OTHER DEER.

STALKING THE SAMBUR — ITS ENEMIES — ITS HABITS — ALARM NOTE — SIZE — TENACITY OF LIFE — HORNS — THEIR VARIABILITY — DEATH OF THE BIG ANTLER STAG—THE PULNEY STAG—TOM SAYERS—THE CROW STAG—THE STAG OF KERENAIG MUND—HIS LAST LEAP—CHECKMATED—DEATH OF THE BLACK CHEETA ROCK STAG—SNOB AND THE STAG—AN EXCITING STALK AND A SAD FINISH—DEATH OF THE BROW ANTLERED STAG—MY LAST STAG—THE AXIS OR SPOTTED DEER—THE JUNGLE SHEEP.

THE Sambur or Sambar, *Cervus aristotelis*[1] is the largest of all the varieties or species of Indian deer. The sight of this grand beast on the mountain side in the early morning before the sun is up makes the pulse beat quicker and intensifies the desire to get within shot and secure the prize; yet patience and perseverance must be the watch words. Look at him cropping the sweet grass at his feet, he hardly takes a mouthful without raising his head and looking around, so wary is he; and well he may be; his enemies are all around him, always on the alert to deprive him of his life; not only has he the native hillman and the English sportsman after him, the one to get him for food in any way he can, the other

[1] Blandford (*l.c.*) says, "why the name *Cervus aristotelis* given to an abnormal horn, has been preferred for the Indian Sámbar, it is difficult to say. The name *C. unicolor* employed by Hamilton Smith is preferable, on account both of priority and suitability, being an appropriate term for the only Indian deer with unspotted young."

to shoot him for the trophy of his head and antlers, but he has still more dreaded enemies watching their opportunities; the subtle tiger springing upon him in his lair; the leopard dropping on him from the branch of a tree as he passes underneath; or a pack of wild dogs chasing him to his death. I have often watched the movements of a sambur on leaving the shola for his evening meal, when suddenly coming across the track of a tiger which has skulked out a few minutes previously; he will at once stop and with arched back, head upraised and every hair of his body erect, utter the peculiar sound which gives all his tribe warning, that an enemy is abroad. This peculiar bell, given by a sambur when either crossing the track of, or seeing a tiger, is a note of alarm apparently instinctive to all the deer tribe. One hot day in August, I was at the Zoological Gardens in London, and all the deer were lying down in the covered sheds; not one was out in the yards. Being anxious to see the samburs which I heard had been bred in the gardens, I imitated this peculiar "tiger bell" as I call it. In less than two minutes, not only were the samburs, but all other deer of every kind, including our red deer, out in the yards with head and tail erect, expressions of alarm in their eyes, and walking as it were on tip toe, looking out for the supposed danger.

Stalking a sàmbur in India must not be compared with stalking the red deer in Scotland. The sambur lives all the day in small woods, sholas as they are called, which abound on the hills, only coming out to feed at early dawn or late evening. These Indian sholas are composed of trees and jungles, giving shade and comparative safety all the day, and thus the stalk can only take place at two stated periods, viz., at earliest morn or at late eve; at other times the sholas must be beaten by men and dogs.

The colour of the sambur when he is at his best, is a very dark brown; some of them get very fat, and the hinds and young stags are fair food for the table. The size varies according to age; a large stag in his prime will stand fourteen hands at the shoulder and weigh over thirty stone. This deer is extremely tenacious of life, much more so according to my experience, than the red deer of the Highlands of Scotland. I have known them hold on for a long time after receiving wounds which would have proved fatal much sooner with the latter species.

McMaster gives an extract from the journal of the Old Forest Ranger, in which he states a case of a stag receiving ten 1-oz. balls before he fell. Two, which he received at first without slackening his speed, passed clean through his body, about the centre of his ribs; after this he ran about a mile, and laid up in a wooded ravine to which he was tracked, and two more balls hit him, one ball breaking his hind leg and another, entering above the rump, passed along the back-bone and came out near the shoulder. He was lost for about an hour, and when he again broke cover two more balls were planted close behind the shoulder, but still he went away strong. In the chase which followed he was hit twice in the body and at last brought down by a ball through his neck when in the act of leaping a rivulet. He, however, got upon his legs again, and stood at bay in the water, and had to have another ball in his head to finish him. He further says that he could quote a dozen instances of the extraordinary tenacity of life possessed by this animal.

The antlers of the sambur vary considerably, both in

length, spread and thickness. In central India they are, as a rule, larger than those of the southern districts. I believe the largest recorded, measured forty-eight inches,[1] but antlers of from thirty-five to thirty-eight inches are magnificent trophies; the largest pair I possess are forty-one and a half inches long, thirty-eight and a half inches spread, beam six and three quarters in girth half way up the horn, and eight and a half inches in girth at the base. The brow antler also varies much in length. The horns of the sambur almost invariably have three tines on each, but an abnormal small tine is occasionally found.

I have recorded in my journals, between 1855 and 1869 the deaths of two hundred and ninety-five sambur; some of the finest of these stags I had known for two or three years before I was able to obtain their heads as trophies. I used to amuse myself by giving them names, and the following extracts from the journals describe the deaths of some of the finest.

A cold frosty morning was that of the 18th of December, 1857, and the sun was still in bed when I peered over the crags down into Nield Field. The telescope travelled slowly over the long green slopes, every nook and corner was carefully examined; "not a thing out," I exclaimed, as I rose up and shut up the glass. Francis, however, did not rise, but shading his eyes with his hand gazed intently at something out in the Field. "Look," he said, "at the foot of that rhododendron tree beyond the open ridge of the hill below, and you will see such a stag!" It took me some time to find the

[1] Blandford (*l.c.*) mentions these, but says "the girth at mid-beam was only 6 inches, others not so long have had a girth 8.25 inches half way up the beam, and 8.5 in horns 41 inches long."

spot as the slope of the hill hid the stag's body, but when I did I beheld a pair of antlers the sight of which gave me quite a thrill and made my heart beat quicker; we both agreed that we had never seen such a splendid head. There was no time to lose, a hasty glance over the ground showed that we could get to the top of the open spur of the hill below us without being seen, the stag would then be not more than ninety yards from us. After an exciting scramble down the rocky crags immediately below us, Francis at one time almost giving up in despair, we got under cover of the spur, when two hinds on a distant hill began belling loudly (probably at a tiger), and fearing they would disturb the stag I hastened up the slope, just in time to behold a hind disappearing into the wood from near where I had last seen the stag; a sickening feeling of "too late!" came over me, but only for a moment, for at the next glance I saw the grand old fellow still lying in his couch, unconscious of danger. Aiming at the junction of his neck and shoulders, I turned him over down the slope, but after a few struggles, he rose and dashed away; the ball from the other barrel struck him a slanting shot in the shoulder; still on he dashed towards the great forest, when a ball from my other rifle caught him behind the ear, sending him a clean somersault, and causing us no little anxiety about the fate of his splendid antlers. It was only on going up to him that we fully realised their beauty and size, and I felt that every hair of my beard was tingling with delight. Francis says he never saw such a big headed stag, and I believe it was really the largest that has ever been killed on these hills; I thought he would never leave off saying "Kaisa-burra-burra sing," "what great antlers." He was in first rate condition, and as near as I could make him, he stood fourteen hands at the shoulder, here is the sketch and measurement of the head and antlers. My last shot had caught him in the ear going right into his brain, rather a lucky one, for even with Bevis I

MEASUREMENTS OF THE ANTLERS IN INCHES.

a—g 41½ inches. b—h 38¾. h—f 13¾, brow antler. e—g 12, brow antler. c—g 36. d—h 34½. k—l 38½. i—j 34¼. m—e and o—h 8 (circumference). g—r 6¾ (circumference). s—t 7¼. w—g 8½ circumference at base, right antler. 8¾ circumference, left antler. The middle or thinnest part of the shaft a circumference of 6½ inches.

might have lost him in such an immense forest; those neck shots are always so uncertain.

Big stags are scarce on the Pulney mountains and I

only killed one whose head I thought worthy of bringing to England. I saw him feeding on a hill side a long way off; when I got about the third of the way down, keeping well out of sight under the spurs of the mountain; to my intense disgust I heard a sambur belling to my right and saw a hind bolting away over the hill, where she stood and belled several times. I shook my fist at her and abused her, not loudly but deeply, making certain she would alarm the stag as he was quite within earshot. However, she moved away and I stole down the hill. It was very noisy work, getting through the dry fern and leafy scrub, but fortunately on the hill side, where I had seen the stag, there was but little of it; I dared not show myself and fully expected when I crossed over the ridge, to find that he had made himself scarce; my delight was consequently great, when I beheld him feeding quite unconcernedly about ninety yards off. He was stern towards me, so I tried a raking shot; perhaps I ought to have waited for him to turn, but he might have fled out of my sight and that tiresome old hind might have begun belling again, so it was well to make sure of him while I had the chance. A loud thud told that I had struck him, and another shot from the left barrel as he dashed across sent him staggering along. I ran forward and saw him standing on the edge of a precipice, and the next moment he fell over with a crash. Alas, for his antlers! There was another stag far down below that looked in astonishment at his rolling brother. I ought to have left him alone, but I could not resist having a crack at him. The second shot was a running one, and my man afterwards said I had broken the deer's hind leg as he went lame, but he did not appear to me to be so, and as he went away far down the mountain I did not follow him. I looked along the track where the first stag had fallen for broken antlers, finding none I hoped they were all right, but when I got down to him I found that one was snapped off at the centre of the beam, and the other had half the upper tine gone. I walked back and picked up the broken antlers and part of the broken tine, so was able to mend them. The head is not equal to many of my Nielgherry stags, but still it is a handsome trophy; he had fallen down from sixty to eighty feet and was a good deal knocked about and bones broken. My first shot had hit him near the hip joint and the other near the point of the shoulder.

There was a stag which frequented the sholas near Peermund which, from his fighting propensities, I named Tom Sayers; he had very massive antlers and I was keen to have them. After killing the leopard, the description of which will be found in the chapter on tigers, I was wending my way to the bungalow, quite satisfied with my morning's sport, when on the crest of the opposite hill appeared a fine stag. I knew him at once as he descended the hill towards me; he was making for the big wood from which I had just emerged, so skirting along the edge under cover of the rhododendron trees, I made haste to meet him. I had got as far as I could without showing myself, and was doubting in my own mind whether he had not given me the slip, when suddenly I saw his massive antlers appearing beyond some detached rhododendrons; on he came walking towards me quite unaware of danger, and when about ninety yards distant, I took him, and gave him both barrels. He turned and dashed away into a patch of high fern. I knew he had got both shots, and on running through the fern

I saw him making for the stream below in a dying state; he staggered on and fell dead in a clump of reed bamboos at the edge of the stream; a huge stag with the most massive antlers I have ever seen. My first shot had struck him at the point of the left shoulder and the second behind the right shoulder, both deadly wounds. When the people went to fetch in the meat in the afternoon they said a leopard had been feeding on the carcass. I went out to watch for him in the evening, but he did not show himself.

On the 22nd January, 1869, I was out in the early morning, and in passing over some ground where I had burned the grass, found fresh tracks of elephants. I measured the circumference of the largest foot print and made it sixty-five and a half inches, this multiplied by two gives the height of the elephant, ten feet eleven inches; as it was doubtful when the tracks had been made, we passed on to the sambur ground, and came on fresh tracks of ibex with those of either a tiger or a large panther, and shortly after my shikarie, Francis, pointed out two sambur by the side of a large wood, and one appeared to be a handsome stag. I had a long stalk down to them, and in the meantime they moved into a dip between two woods. Whilst watching them, a crow settled on the antlers of the large one and kept cawing as if warning him of my approach; however, the stag did not appear to understand crow language, for on my crossing over the side of the hill the crow was gone but the stag was standing quite unalarmed about eighty yards away from me. Part of him was hidden by a tree, but a step on one side uncovered his shoulder, and the next moment I had pitched him apparently right on his head, Francis screaming with delight, but the stag was up again as quick as he fell and dashed through the wood; I ran as fast as I could to intercept him, and was putting in a fresh cartridge as I ran, when out hė came about hundred yards distant; I fired a hurried shot without stopping him, and

THE UNHEEDED WARNING.

as he appeared to be so strong, and finding a good deal of blood on his tracks, and as he had gone up a dip into another wood, I sent off for the dogs. The wood we tracked him into was a small one, so I posted myself and sent Francis through on the blood track; to my disappointment the deer had gone on, but instead of entering the large forest beyond, the track skirted it and lead down a very steep hill, the blood spots gradually getting less and less. The dogs soon arrived, the two Australian kangaroo dogs and Victor, a half hound half blood hound; telling the men only to slip the dogs if the stag got up, I waited the result, and my hopes fell when Francis made signs that the track continued down the hill towards the river. I stalked along the bank hoping the stag might be in the water, but saw no signs of him, only very fresh tracks of a tiger on the sand.

Beyond the river there were two immense forests. We had entirely lost the track, but after hunting for a long time I found one spot of blood where the deer had entered the stream in the direction of one of the woods, and although I could not find any blood on the other bank to distinguish the track of the wounded deer from many others, I concluded he had made for the wood, but after hunting up nearly all of them without success, I went back again to the stream and after infinite trouble found a footstep with one unmistakeable drop of blood leading to a detached wood. My excitement was great as I stole round to command the upper part, but I was again to be disappointed. They found where the stag had lain down and tracked him out of it in the direction of another very small wood. I posted myself at the top, listening for the slightest sound; presently I heard a voice and a whistle and hastened down; the boy with the two Australian dogs had started the stag which had doubled back, yet the idiot had never loosed the dogs. As soon as I got on the track I gave orders for the dogs to be let go, but I was in utter despair, for instead of their taking up the scent, they tore about in all directions in the wildest manner possible. I then sent one of the men to a hill top to look out while I endeavoured to take up the track; presently the look out made signs, and I hastened up to him; he had seen two of the dogs in chase of a deer far away on the opposite side of a deep and densely wooded ravine, too far off to tell if it was a stag, but he said the deer went as if crippled; the only spark of hope was that they were coming back in our direction and not going away from us. After waiting a short time not knowing exactly what to do, there was a rush in the wood below us, and to my great delight out came the stag with two of the dogs at his flank, I saw he was quite done and was making down the open hill side for the stream below. He dashed into it and stood at bay; stalking carefully down I put a ball behind the shoulder and thus ended one of the most exciting day's sport I have had for a long while. To show how strong these big stags are, I may mention that my first shot had entered near the point of the shoulder, passed through the lower part of the chest, and through the opposite leg below the elbow, without breaking the bone. I fired my my first shot at him about eight o'clock a.m., and brought him to bay about a quarter to three p.m. The variations between hope and despair during the day were great, but the finish was fine.

One morning, when at Kerenaig-mund, I went out soon after dawn to the Neild Field, in hopes of meeting with a fine stag which frequented it. The morning was beautifully clear, but it soon came on to blow half a gale of wind and not a sambur was out; I watched till half past nine then had my breakfast, and was out in the field again at half past two. Nothing came out; and as I was cogitating on my bad luck I suddenly saw the spreading antlers of a noble stag appear on the other side of the slope about fifty paces from me; he stood staring at me, I could only see his head and half his neck, but I aimed through the grass at his chest, he turned back and was out of sight in an instant, but the thud of the bullet was loud and unmistakable. I ran up the slope but no stag was visible; the ground below appeared too precipitous for him to have gone straight back. At last after a long search we discovered his track with quantities of

HIS LAST LEAP.

blood. We followed it up and found he had gone at speed over a perpendicular rock with a sheer drop of at least fifty feet, but from the hill being so steep the distance he had gone through the air before reaching the ground was a great deal more; we found him some hundred yards further down firmly jammed in the middle of a small clump of bushes. I fully expected that his antlers would have been smashed to pieces, but they fortunately were quite uninjured, and very fine ones they were with a grand spread of thirty-eight inches and the same in length; the beams very massive.

One morning as I was proceeding to the lower part of the middle crags Francis pointed out a fine stag feeding under the cliffs, so we immediately started to stalk him. I got to the cliff above him and as I craned over, I saw him looking at me. I had to fire right down on his back, and as he dashed away I gave him the other barrel. He pulled up a long way out of shot, turned round and deliberately looked at us. With the glass I could see quite plainly, two wounds—one on the withers and the other evidently a flesh wound on the fore arm—there he stood, every now and again raising his injured leg and afraid to move. He had taken up a very commanding position on the spur of the mountain, and after watching him for a quarter of an hour I left Francis to occupy his attention while I endeavoured to stalk up to him from below. However, it was such a still evening that he could hear every rustle of the grass as I approached, and long before I got within fair shot he saw me, and I had to remain where I was for more than half an hour, regularly checkmated. At last he disappeared over the brow, and I was immediately up and after him, but he had gone down the mountain and I saw him far down below us close to the forest, going uncommonly strong for a wounded one. He was a very large stag, as Francis said, like a buffalo, with handsome horns; it was disappointing not getting him, and I was by no means pleased with my shooting; however, there is this to be said that shots from above are more likely than any others to glance and miss the vital parts.

I was anxious to get a stag which I had known for some time, and which frequented a small wood at the foot of a precipitous rock, so one cold frosty morning in January, 1869,

I started to find him. I did not succeed in getting a stalk, so put my men through one or two small woods, posting myself at the likely spots for the deer to break cover. I was proceeding to one of these points when I was told a stag had been seen standing at the edge of the wood, which he had entered without my seeing him. I ran round the top to intercept him, on which he quietly trotted out at the bottom, "a fine handsome beastie," as a Scotch keeper would say, I at once recognised him to be the stag I was after and one that had dodged us out of the very same wood some time before; he seemed now to be making for a wood at the foot of the precipitous rock. The first black leopard I ever saw came out of this wood and sat in the open washing his face with his paws, like an old black tom cat before the fire, so I named the rock after him. Seeing that the stag was making for this cover I concluded he would in all probability lay up there. I had a pony out with me so I tied him up near the run by which the deer had entered, and ordered the men to walk through the top; but there was one difficulty to be overcome; the wind was blowing right into the wood; if I posted myself at the lower and most likely spot for the deer to break cover, he would be sure to have my wind and not come out that way. I therefore tried a stratagem. Walking along close to the wood I stood at one spot letting him thoroughly wind me, and when I judged he knew exactly where I was standing I stole back the way I came and made a long detour to a pass higher up the hill. The men had orders to enter the wood from above and commence clapping their hands as soon as they saw me posted; presently out trotted a smaller stag some distance up the hill above me; he stood and looked at me and gave a tempting shot, but I held my hand, hoping the big one would follow. I waited, but there was no sign of him so turned down the hill again rather regretting I had let the small stag go, when I suddenly caught sight of the head and spreading antlers of the big stag perfectly motionless in some thick scrub near the edge of the wood; he was evidently watching me, thinking he was unseen, and I am pretty sure he had sent out the smaller stag as a feeler! There was no time to lose; he was about

PUZZLED.

a hundred and thirty yards off with only his head and neck visible, so taking a steady aim I let drive, heard a loud tell, and the stag wheeled round and disappeared. I made the men beat up to me, when there was a rush and out came, not the stag, but a hind; I then posted one of the men outside and took up the track from where the stag stood: had some difficulty in finding it, as there was so little blood at first, but it soon increased and I had not gone far when I heard the stag get up and move away. I rushed out and saw him making tracks back to the wood I had first started him from, but fortunately I had picketed my pony on the line, and the sight of him puzzled the stag and brought him to a standstill, giving me a long shot, which told and turned him back into the wood; but as he appeared to be very strong I sent for the dogs and my breakfast. It must have been nearly three o'clock before they arrived; I first satisfied my hunger and then took up the track. The dogs soon began to pull eagerly, so I let them go, and had the satisfaction of hearing

SNOB AND THE STAG.

them and the stag rushing through the wood. It was not long before they brought him to bay in the scrub where I had my first shot at him; it was very thick, and I had difficulty in getting to him. When I did so I found that another shot was not required. The knife soon put him out of his misery. My first shot had struck him beyond the right shoulder travelling back; the second in the hip.

My dog Snob was very keen for going in at the stags and pinning them by the nose. A small horned stag came stepping out the mund, whilst I was waiting at the end of a shola about eighty yards below; he caught sight of me and stood broadside on. The next instant he was thrown on his tracks with a ball high up in his shoulder. Snob had put him up and ran in at him immediately he fell. The deer struggled violently and got up with Snob hanging on his nose, but he soon fell again, to Snob's intense satisfaction. Poor old Snob! he was one of the pluckiest dogs I ever possessed. He came to a sad end from the bite of a leopard, and was a great loss to me.

I was out at Peer-mund on the 23rd of February, 1867, when Francis came to say a big stag was coming up the hill, so I hastened out of the shola and from "the future Avalanche" I saw a fine stag; he was a good way down but evidently making for the shola I had just left. The wind had lulled a good deal so there was not much fear of his getting our wind, but his caution was very great. He would stop every few yards, look steadily ahead, and occasionally smell the ground. As he came zigzagging up the hill, I admired through the glass his fine, thick, well beaded antlers, with thick and long, brow antlers. The only defect was that the upper tines were rather too small for the mass of antler, but it was a beautiful head. I tried to guess the length of horn and put it down as above thirty-five inches; on he came; there was only one pass under the perpendicular rock to the shola, so taking off our shoes we hastened down to the plateau of the lower rocks; I told Francis that the moment the stag came to where we had been down below, he would smell our track and bolt, however, we could command the spot from the top of the cliffs. When we got there the stag was approaching our track, and directly he got on to it, he threw up his head; I whispered to Francis that I must fire at once or he would be off; he was about one hundred and

NOW BOUNDING INTO THE AIR.

twenty yards below me, standing three quarters on. I took a steady shot at him but could not say whether I hit; he wheeled about but had only gone a short distance when I gave him the contents of the other barrel and then a ball from the carbine. We saw that the latter had broken his fore leg, and that he was evidently hard hit besides; he stood holding his broken leg in the air, but struggled on again down the hill. I gave him another couple of shots, one of these I saw went over his back. He had got a good way down by this time and was very much crippled. However, Francis handed me another rifle and asked me to "maro," so I fired two more shots, one struck just in front of him, the other we heard strike; he was now apparently quite done for, so I said it was no use firing any more and hastened down. As I turned a corner I heard a rattling of stones, and to my intense dismay saw this splendid antlered stag rolling like a large rock down the side of the mountain over crag and precipice; now bounding into the air, now disappearing over a rock to be seen again far below amidst a shower of stones and dust. Oh, dear! oh, dear! he will not have a bit of antler left, and he won't stop till he gets down into the low country! It certainly looked as if he would never stop rolling, but fortunately a slight ridge stopped him quite on the edge of the last precipice. If he had got over this he would have gone right down; as it was he fell nearly a thousand feet. We followed his track down and picked up two pieces of antler. When we got to him we found his head smashed to pieces, so much so that one of the eyes was in the brain, and there was nothing but the stumps of his glorious antlers left. Five shots had struck him. We hunted up his track again and found five pieces of antler including the two upper tines, but there was a great deal wanting and from the appearance on the rocks I think some parts of the horns must have been pounded to dust. He was a very fat stag, so after taking what we could carry we covered up the remainder with grass, as Francis said the people would come for the meat, but there were some hungry vultures watching us.

I was on the Nielgherries on December 9th, 1869, but I hardly expected a good stag would fall to my rifle this morning, for I had been unfortunate with a fine fellow I had seen at peep o' day; he either winded or heard me, and was soon over the hills and far away. It then set in misty with a drizzling rain which put a stop to stalking. However, I thought I would send the two men to walk through a long strip of shola that occasionally harboured a deer, so posting myself near the top I awaited the result. The men had nearly reached me when I heard a movement in the wood close to me. I was not at all sure it might not be one of the men, when suddenly the horns and head of the well known brow antlered stag appeared not thirty yards from me. He instantly saw me and stood; as instantly I sent him rolling back into the wood and he was "gathered to his fathers." A well shaped head, with very thick fine brow antlers. I had known him for some years, but had not seen him often. He had evidently been fighting desperately during the night and had a great gash and a stab in his throat and two or three prods in his face. As he had no hind with him I conclude he lost the fight. May I come across the victor!

I killed my last sambur on the 10th February, 1871, at the Avalanche, Nielgherries. I saw a fine stag with a hind lying down on the slopes about one hundred yards below me. They saw me, but allowed me to change the carbine for the Toy rifle without getting up. I took a very deliberate shot at the stag, heard the hit, but he galloped down the side of the mountain as if untouched; I fired the other barrel but the ball went just over his back; he disappeared under the hill, when suddenly I heard a tremendous crash in the shola, and Francis said he had just seen him fall over. The hind appeared below and did not seem to know where to go without him. I found the stag lying in the stony water-course, having fallen over a sheer rock of some twenty feet

THE DEER STALKER.

without injuring his antlers beyond a scrape or two; had he fallen on his back he must have smashed them all to pieces. A very handsome head, the smaller antler had a little extra point on the upper tine. He was a very large stag in bulk, looking, as Francis said, like a bullock. I had struck him just in the right place behind the shoulder the ball passing through and lodging in the hind fetlock which was underneath him. This stag was the one I had been after for the last two years. On one occasion I missed him; on another he came over the hill with two hinds and a young stag when he "did me" by crossing on the other side too far for a certain shot. I named him "Sir Charles" after my friend Sir Charles Trevelyan.

One of the most beautiful denizens of the Indian Forest is the Axis or Spotted Deer (*Axis maculata, Cervus axis*). All Southern Indian sportsmen love the pursuit of these graceful "dappled beauties;" it leads them amongst some of the most characteristic scenery of hill and plain, as well as the bamboo jungles and their verdant glades, and although he cannot be compared with the lordly sambur as an object of sport, still there is a peculiar attraction in the glossy bright and spotted hide of the buck cheetul. I first became acquainted with them in the Dandilly Forest in 1844 and came across many a herd. We shot a fair number, but I had the misfortune to lose a very grand buck. We had been out after bison, and had just crossed a nullah when we saw a large herd of spotted deer feeding a long way off. The shikarie told me to go on by myself which I did. There were some splendid bucks with the herd. When some thirty yards off, one of them with magnificent antlers saw me; fearing that he would give the alarm, I let drive at him, and down he came on his knees, but was up again and away with a broken thigh. I dashed after him and came up to him hobbling away very slowly, but before I could get another fair shot he had disappeared in the jungle, and although we tracked him for more than a mile I never saw him again. These deer are at times most difficult to see in the jungle. In this instance after giving up the wounded buck, the shikarie pointed out another herd, in which he said there was a "sing walla" (a fine buck). I could see one or two does offering tempting shots but I would not fire, and they moved on, and then to my disgust I saw that what I had taken for the stump of a tree about seventy yards from me, was the white chest and neck of the buck.

In June, 1864, I went to join my friend Falkner on a sporting trip, and devoted myself entirely to the pursuit of the spotted Deer, and whilst on this trip I shot some very good bucks, with fine heads. One had antlers thirty-one and three quarter inches in length with a spread of twenty-three inches, another thirty-four and a quarter inches long with a spread of twenty-one inches, and another thirty-one and a quarter in length with a spread of twenty-six inches; the average length in Southern India being a little under thirty inches. All these were very handsome animals, the horns being very massive and beautifully shaped. Coming home that evening in the dusk, we had just entered a glade when the Punnian pointed, and I saw what I thought was a very large spotted buck. I fired at it, but there it remained, and when I went up to it I found it was a bush with white leaves! In this trip I killed a spotted deer with very extraordinary antlers. I found a herd in an open glade, with two very fine bucks. I got down to them and was just going to fire at what I thought was the largest of the two when he laid down behind a bush and I could only see the top of his antlers. The other buck looked very large so I determined to have a crack at him. I threw him on his tracks about fifty-five yards distant. He bellowed like a bull, and on going up I found he had the most extraordinary antlers I ever saw. No less than ten tines. The length of the antlers were thirty-three and a half inches

THE AXIS, OR SPOTTED DEER.

and the spread twenty-five and a half—a fine massive, well beaded head, thick enough for a sambur.

EXTRAORDINARY ANTLERS.

The Ribfaced Deer or Barking Deer, or Jungle Sheep as it is called in Southern India (the name being derived from the word Jungli-bakri,) *Cervulus muntjac*, often fell to my rifle, shot chiefly for food for myself and the men. Its bark is very peculiar, something like that of the wild dog, and at times very loud, particularly before going to couch. I have often wondered how so small an animal could make this peculiar roar or bark, when alarmed or otherwise. The long canines in the jaw are not firmly fixed but are very moveable, and they appear to be quite under control of the animal so that they can be moved to different angles and thus be made formidable weapons of defence, and I have had my dogs severely wounded by these scimitar like teeth. I at one time thought that this peculiar bark was produced, or rather helped, by these teeth, probably assisted by its long tongue, but I have doubts as to whether I am right as to this. The male certainly makes at times a rattling kind of noise as if two pieces of loose bones were hit together or more like a pair of castanets. The natives say that this peculiar noise is only made when the muntjack crosses the fresh track of a tiger.

THE JUNGLE SHEEP.

INDEX.